# time
## *smart*

# time
## *smart*

### *How to* RECLAIM YOUR TIME
### & LIVE A HAPPIER LIFE

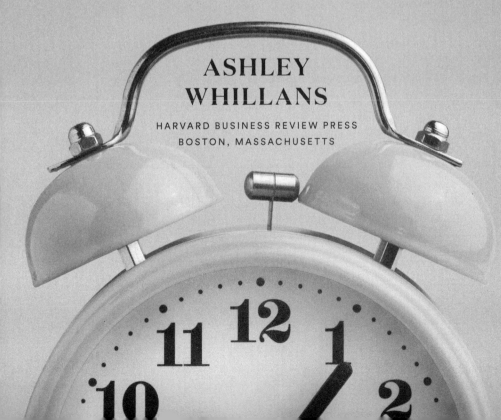

ASHLEY
WHILLANS

HARVARD BUSINESS REVIEW PRESS
BOSTON, MASSACHUSETTS

Library of Congress Cataloging-in-Publication Data

Names: Whillans, Ashley V., author.
Title: Time smart : how to reclaim your time and live a happier life / Ashley Whillans.
Description: Boston. MA : Harvard Business Review Press, [2020] | Includes index.
Identifiers: LCCN 2020012312 (print) | LCCN 2020012313 (ebook) | ISBN 9781633698352 (hardcover) | ISBN 9781633698369 (ebook)
Subjects: LCSH: Time management. | Happiness.
Classification: LCC HD69.T54 W46 2020 (print) | LCC HD69.T54 (ebook) | DDC 650.1/1—dc23
LC record available at https://lccn.loc.gov/2020012312
LC ebook record available at https://lccn.loc.gov/2020012313

ISBN: 978-1-63369-835-2
eISBN: 978-1-63369-836-9

For my partner, my family, and my friends,
all of whom have taught me
the true value of time.

# CONTENTS

# time
## *smart*

# the art and science of being time smart

Time and money. They share a lot in common: both are measurable, and both are scarce. Both are what most of us would say are the most valuable *things* we can have. We want more time and we want more money, and we work to get them.

But as young adults, we learn quickly that for all their similarities, time and money are set against each other, and it seems to stay that way for the rest of our working lives. It's difficult to gain as much of both as we want. Mostly, we're choosing between them, making trade-offs. The old aphorism—if you have the money you don't have the time, and if you have the time you don't have the money—seems true. Over and over we find ourselves choosing between time and money. Cook or eat out? Work or go on vacation? Find a second job or spend more time with the kids?

I became fascinated with the trade-offs people make between time and money when I was a PhD student, in part because a PhD student's life is a conscious choice to trade money for time, to spend years becoming an expert on new ideas with very little financial reward. To quell my curiosity, I surveyed thousands of working adults around the world—from Danish millionaires to working parents and single moms living day by day in the United States, East Africa, and India—about these two very simple, universally valuable resources: time and money.

What surprised me most about people's answers was the disconnect between how important many of these time and money decisions were and how trivial they seemed in the moment. These trade-offs are so seemingly dull or obvious, we often don't even realize we're making them. Again and again in my research, and in my life (because once you start paying attention to this topic, you can't escape it; it's the lens through which you see people and their choices), I've heard stories about the decisions people make about time and money. These stories show that these decisions sneak up on us, and that any given choice—whether it's a big decision like what career to choose or a tiny decision like whether to use those last two vacation days—seems to be inconsequential and easy to reverse. But it is not. All these decisions powerfully shape the happiness we derive from moments, from days, from our entire lives.

These decisions affect everyone—not only the financially affluent. If anything, people with fewer means have more to gain by thinking critically about how they make decisions about time and money. Some of the examples I discuss in this book involve professionals and the well-to-do—including millionaires—but others illustrate the trade-offs faced by single moms in developing countries who are living day by day. I also share stories of companies helping diverse groups of people effectively navigate time and money trade-offs—from Silicon Valley companies offering computer engineers housecleaning services to a startup helping the poorest Americans save time by transforming their commutes. In my research, almost everyone, from CEOs to students to working parents, face trade-offs between time and money and can improve their decision making in the moments when they choose.

## Time and Money in Daily Life

Several stories from my research stick with me as prototypical of those facing time and money decisions.

Nicole was a newly minted executive at a major credit card company. Thomas, her husband, was a busy VP. They were rarely in the same city and hadn't taken a vacation together in years. One day, Thomas received a pleasant surprise: courtesy of a generous client, he was offered the chance to extend his work trip by a week and enjoy the Swiss Alps, all expenses paid. This was a once-in-a-lifetime opportunity. Thomas pleaded with his wife. "Nicole, please come. It's only for a few days." Nicole sighed and said, "I can't. I have an important meeting that I shouldn't miss." Thomas hit the slopes with his sister Leah instead, and the siblings enjoyed what they both deemed "the best trip ever."

"Five years later, they still talk about this damn trip," Nicole told me. "And, whenever they do, Thomas asks me, 'Nicole, what was that meeting about again?' 'To be honest, I can't remember.' He always replies, 'That important, huh?'"

Later, Nicole admitted that she had vacation time available, and the meeting was optional. Her team would have been fine without her. But at the time, it seemed too important to her; she just felt she should be there. Thomas and Leah made memories that will last a lifetime, while Nicole's "important" work obligations have faded into the past.

During a recent field visit in rural India, fifteen-year-old Usha explained to me the daily decision she has to make: spend time getting and transporting water (in large, heavy urns balanced on her head) to support her family, *or* attend school. "I have to fetch water from wells and ponds, which takes hours every day and leaves me no time to attend school. I want to be a teacher, but I do not have time to study because of these chores, which are killing my dreams. Without help, I will live a life of poverty—filled with unknown darkness and illiteracy." Although most of our lives are very different from Usha's, many working parents

I have talked to feel a similar tension between supporting their families (versus working more hours, or going back to school). Society needs to help Ushas everywhere feel that they have the time and support to choose school over chores.

Another story that's never far from my mind is that of Alice, a first-generation college student. She paid her own way through school and worked her way up from research assistant to PhD. After graduation, she was lucky enough to be offered two jobs that could be classified as dream jobs. Job 1 offered reasonable hours, social connection, and meaning. It would allow her to live in her hometown, surrounded by friends and family. She wouldn't make much money but would contribute her skills to the community by working for local government. Job 2 offered money and prestige. It required a cross-country move to a new city. Alice would be given more opportunities than she ever imagined, having grown up the daughter of a mail carrier in a small town.

She chose job 2 without much hesitation. At that time, it seemed like a no-brainer. Alice and her partner of eight years, Paul, didn't have kids. It would be the adventure of a lifetime, and hard work now would lead to many opportunities later. Except when they settled in, Paul was miserable. Alice traveled a lot, and Paul had no job and no friends to turn to. After three months he moved home, and they parted ways forever. Alice was devastated, but under contract. All she could do was keep working.

Later that year, while Alice was working overseas, her best friend had her first child. Then Alice's cousin passed away. The funeral was scheduled at the same time as a work trip. Alice told herself what many of us tell ourselves when we sacrifice our time for jobs and money: "It's fine. I'm doing this now so I will have more time to be happy tomorrow, and I can make it up to people then."

This logic makes sense, as long as tomorrow actually arrives. It didn't for Carly and Adam, who were happy, healthy, and productive thirty-somethings living in Oregon. Adam was a teacher. Carly was finishing grad school. On the weekends, they hiked near their house and cooked meals for the week. Adam was training for his first marathon. Carly started outdoor climbing. They shared an apartment, adopted a puppy, and began saving for a wedding (and kids!). They were busy—always too busy to go on the dream road trip they had planned but kept putting off until next year.

Just before Carly was to graduate, Adam was rushed to the ER with cramps and a fever. It seemed like appendicitis. Shockingly, Adam and Carly learned that Adam had advanced pancreatic cancer, and three months to live. Within twenty-four hours, Carly and Adam were married. Carly quit school and set in motion a road trip cum honeymoon across the Pacific Northwest that the couple would schedule in between chemo treatments. On their GoFundMe page, Carly wrote, "We thought we had all the time in the world."

No matter our age, education, or income, we share the same reality: none of us knows how much time we have left. One day, time runs out and tomorrow never comes. This is one of the core discoveries I've made researching time and money: we don't understand well that time is our most valuable resource, and it is finite. Chasing money is valuable to a point, but it's an infinite errand. You can always try to get more—and research shows people do that, no matter how much money they have already. Given how precious time is, we should put it first. But many of us focus on our careers, constantly giving up more of our time in exchange for more money or productivity.

We're conditioned to do this. Since the Industrial Revolution, we've learned to put a dollar value on time. We've been told, literally, that money is our most valuable resource: time is money. To gain financial prosperity we've exchanged things that make us happy, at great expense. Many twenty- and thirty-year-olds like Alice sacrifice the best years of their lives based on the assumption that they can make time for joy tomorrow. I can attest to this. If you hadn't yet figured it out, I am Alice.

Meanwhile, those in their thirties and forties chase the idea of having perfect children and careers, deferring personal and marital bliss until they retire. They can take the transformative vacation in the Alps when they're older and more settled.

Then fifty-, sixty-, and seventy-year-olds continue to work, putting off life goals and bucket-list items until "next year," year after year—only to run out of time and end up, like my friend's dad, with unused plane tickets lining the inside of their caskets.

This sounds heavy, and it is. My research has shown me that the stakes really are this high. People tend to focus too much on working and making money and not enough on having more and better time. Most of us, myself included, fail to value time as much as money. This focus on money contributes to the epidemic levels of stress, unhappiness, and loneliness that many societies struggle with. It costs us a lot, financially and otherwise. Collectively researchers call this phenomenon *time poverty*, and it is chronic.

## The Shape of This Book

Throughout this book you will calculate trade-offs between time and money, and see that many of the decisions you make are suboptimal. It's easy to make time choices poorly, and easier still to underestimate the long-term costs of prioritizing money. Just as analytics in sports have transformed how teams are built, the analytics that expose the flaws in time–money decision making—along with some understanding of the psychological and behavioral biases that drive us—will help reshape our choices about how we build our lives.

That doesn't mean the choices are always easy and obvious. It has become clear to me in the course of my research that there's no one right way of approaching time–money decisions. For example, I can't say for certain whether Nicole made the right decision, only that, in general, data suggest that she would have been happier making a different one. We all want different things in life, and each of us wants different things at different times in our lives. The best choice will vary. And society prevents some people, like Usha, from making better choices. That's where policy makers need to better recognize the value of time.

Still, we know that for a large number of people, at all economic strata and across many cultures, the best choices are not being made.

Nothing less than our health and our happiness depends on reversing the nearly innate notion that time is money. It's not. *Money is time.* This book will help you live that truth.

You will start in **Chapter 1, "Time Traps and the Time Poverty Epidemic,"** by delving into how pernicious time poverty can be for anyone, no matter their means.[1] You may be surprised by the costs, in the same way that you may be surprised when you see your cash spending laid out over the course of a year. You might think, *I spend how much on coffee and dining out?!* But unlike those accountings, you'll also look at the startling effects of being time impoverished, from the profound (massively elevated stress) to the peculiar (less smiling).

**Chapter 2, "Steps to Finding Time and Funding Time,"** looks from the other shore at *time affluence*: the state of having and using time meaningfully. Who is time affluent? A few people. What do they do differently? For one, they spend more time eating. And how does time affluence change them? No spoiler: they're much, much happier.

With a newfound understanding, you'll turn to yourself and learn what you can do to recognize and avoid **time traps** that prevent you from achieving time affluence in **chapter 3, "The Time-Affluence Habit."** All of us can become more time affluent without quitting our jobs or winning the lottery. You must commit to time affluence as you do to your physical health, which is the cumulative effect of many small behavior changes such as taking the stairs instead of an elevator and eating a salad for dinner more often than eating a cheeseburger. Similarly, time affluence involves small decisions that allow you to have more and better time, such as saying no more often and paying your way out of time-consuming, unrewarding tasks.

Time affluence, like financial affluence, also involves long-term planning. **Chapter 4, "The Long View,"** lays out strategies to help you plan for longer arcs of time, such as building a career or a family. It will never be enough to change your behavior once and stick with it. Demands change. Goals shift. Life happens. By planning and reevaluating your time choices, you can make decisions based on what you need at different stages.

Finally, you'll turn your attention to other people who influence your time affluence. **Chapter 5, "Systemic Change,"** shows you how systems, from technology to public policy to human resources, work against a time-affluent existence. This chapter lays out intervention strategies to support a better balance between time and money for citizens and employees. Being time affluent is not only good for you as an individual, it is also good for institutions, which often are led by people who have no idea about the negative costs they're accruing because of the time poverty they help perpetuate. It is my hope that you will share this chapter with people in HR and government who have the power to effect change and create time affluence.

In each chapter, you'll get to apply what you've learned by using toolkits that contain activities and worksheets. These toolkits will help you to account for your time and plan ways to recuperate wasted time so that you can climb your way out of time poverty.

## Are You a Taylor or a Morgan?

To get the most from the strategies and activities in this book, it helps to have a baseline understanding of how you think about time and money now. So pause and reflect on how you typically make trade-offs between time and money. Then read the descriptions of the two people that follow, and decide which one you most strongly identify with. It doesn't have to be a perfect match. Just pick who, on average, most closely resembles your outlook and decision making.

> **Taylor** values **time** more than money. Taylor is willing to sacrifice money to have more time. For example, Taylor would rather work fewer hours and make less money than work more hours and make more money.
>
> **Morgan** values **money** more than time. Morgan is willing to sacrifice time to have more money. For example, Morgan would

rather work more hours and make more money than work fewer hours and have more time.

I have presented this activity to tens of thousands of people. Just by knowing whether someone's a Taylor or a Morgan, I can predict behavior with surprising accuracy. I know what kinds of flights they'll choose and what kinds of gifts they value most. I can also predict how many hours they work, if they volunteer, their socializing behaviors, and even what kinds of jobs they'll take. It's not a magic trick; it's only matching data to behaviors.[2] Now that I've done that you will benefit, because the strategies that follow in this book are based on rigorous studies from behavioral science that take into consideration whether you're a Taylor or a Morgan.

So which are you? Spend time thinking about this question, and answer honestly. Calling yourself a Taylor because you think that's more desirable means neither that you actually are a Taylor nor that you're perfectly time affluent. It's possible for you to become more time rich, no matter where you start from. And don't suppose that there is a right answer or that you are inherently one or the other. Sure, some factors make us more inclined to be a Taylor or a Morgan, but it changes many times during our lives. I am a time researcher who understands all the data on time poverty, but if I'm honest with myself, at this point in my life I have to conclude that I am a Morgan.

Because you're reading this book, I suspect you feel like a Morgan, but even if you identify as a Taylor you can benefit from practicing being more time smart. Studies show a wide range of benefits for those who focus on time over money. A time-centric mindset:

- *Promotes happiness.* People gain about half as much happiness from valuing time more than money as they would from being married.[3] And this boost holds across demographics: it's not explained by the amount of money people make, their educational background, the number of kids they have living at home, or their marital status.

- *Promotes social connections.* Focusing on time encourages us to put our social relationships first.[4] Even fleeting social interactions—such as chatting with that person you always see on the bus—can play a surprisingly important role in reducing time stress and increasing happiness.[5]

- *Promotes relationship satisfaction.* Time-focused people have happier spouses and better sex lives than money-focused people. Couples who spend money on time-saving services spend more quality time together and derive greater happiness from their relationships. Time-saving purchases can even erase some of the unhappiness of having an unsupportive spouse. My research suggests that paying for a house cleaner might do as much for your marriage as learning how to be a better listener.[6]

- *Promotes job satisfaction.* People who value time work the same number of hours as people who value money. Ironically, those who value time often make more income than those who value money, because they are more likely to pursue careers they love and so they work with less stress, are more productive and creative, and are less likely to quit.[7]

Most important of all, being time-centric is ***prosocial***, which is the word academics use to describe actions that benefit others.

When you are building your time-affluence toolkit, there could be a moment when it makes you feel guilty.[8] You may think that time affluence is a nice way of saying privilege. You may think, *I can afford to make decisions of time over money, and others can't. I'm being selfish.*

I've struggled with this myself. Friends and colleagues have teased me about my research making life easier for well-off people. Over time, these feelings have gone away, for two reasons. First, we have begun to amass data showing that time affluence positively affects people at all economic strata.[9] Second, studies have emerged showing that the time affluence you gain can benefit everyone, because it puts you in a better position to help others.

When I have to say no, or when I am about to take a vacation, I try to think about the fact that freeing up my time unlocks energy that I can use to invest in the causes and people I care about—such as helping undergraduate students apply for PhD programs or spending time with my partner. This argument isn't merely a hopeful anecdote; it's based on rigorous data: when we feel we have enough time, we're better able to serve others.

The most famous example of time affluence encouraging us to help others is the "Good Samaritan" study. In this study, researchers recruited theology students from Princeton, who completed a couple of questionnaires that—in typical psychology study fashion—were bogus, only a means to an end. The students were then asked to schlep across campus to a local elementary school to teach the story of the Good Samaritan, who helps a downtrodden stranger by the side of the road.

After completing the initial survey, some students were told that they were running late and that the class was already waiting for their arrival. Other students were told they had several minutes to get to class. On their walk across campus, all students encountered a man slumped over in an alley, moaning in pain. Most of the students who were told they had time stopped to help. But fewer than 10 percent of the students who were in a hurry helped the man; most didn't even take notice.[10]

Other research—including some of my own—points to the same general conclusion: people who feel time rich are more likely to volunteer, engage with local politicians, and help out at their kids' school.[11] People who feel time rich are also more likely to be eco-friendly by taking time out of their day to recycle and compost, and by buying energy-efficient appliances.[12]

Even reminding ourselves of the prosocial nature of time can help us make better time decisions. When we think about time-saving purchases as prosocial acts ("these purchases help me spend time with people I care about"), we feel less guilt and are more likely to follow through with those choices.[13]

In short, as you embark on the difficult challenge of prioritizing time over money, remind yourself that focusing on time isn't only about you. By focusing on time, you can contribute to the happiness of family, friends, coworkers, your community, and the planet.

● ● ●

The secret to happier time is simple: prioritize time over money—one decision at a time.

As with many of life's truths, it is easy to know and far more difficult to live. These pages aren't filled with promises of quick and easy transformations. Most of the interventions I write about produce small (but noticeable) increases in time affluence and implementing and executing these changes takes careful thought.

I'm here to help, but living a time-affluent life is ultimately part of a new mindset and new discipline you will develop. The learning never really stops. I still struggle every day with decisions about time and money. I say yes too often when work opportunities arise where the personal costs outweigh the professional benefits. My partner often has to sit me down and say, "Ashley, you should really get out of this. It is not worth your time."

My life is a work in progress. But my research and personal experiences have taught me that time is worth fighting for. None of us knows how much of it we have left. The present, this moment right now, is the best time to start to make small but meaningful changes so that you can be less stressed, enjoy your job more, and have healthier social relationships—so that you can, in short, be time rich and live your best life. Happiness is not the subject of this book. It's the product.

Let's get started.

# 1

# *time traps and the time poverty epidemic*

There is an eight-out-of-ten chance that you are one of the poorest people in the world.[1] When I say you're poor, I'm not talking about your bank account (although material poverty is a pressing concern in society). Rather, I mean you are *time poor*: you have too many things to do and not enough time to do them. In countries as different as the United States, Germany, and Japan, time poverty is at an all-time high.[2]

No one is immune to the crushing feelings of time poverty. As I sit here typing at my kitchen table I, too, feel time poor and overwhelmed. For me, it's a squeezing feeling in my stomach. This morning, a student emailed me requesting urgent help with a paper, preventing me from starting this chapter as soon as I would have liked. Even as I start to write, I keep an eye on my phone. At any moment—*sigh*—a coworker will text me for help with an imminent deadline. I have to stop working early for a doctor's appointment, after which I'll rush home and fumble together a late dinner consisting of salad and whatever, before returning to my inbox and my "rolling to-do list." That's the title of a document I keep open on my laptop. It sprawls for pages.

I can't fit in all the work I need to finish. I will try to shoehorn in a conversation with my partner. I probably won't get a chance to chat with friends. I need to find time to talk to my rapidly aging parents.

Today isn't unusual for me, and it probably sounds familiar to you, too. Time poverty affects all cultures and crosses all economic strata. Most of us feel this way.

## Is It Really That Bad?

Yes, it really is that bad. In 2012, about 50 percent of working Americans reported they were "always rushed," and 70 percent "never" had enough time.[3] In 2015, more than 80 percent said they didn't have the time they needed.[4] That's how I guessed you were time poor. You've said so.

If you're worried that this is some kind of first-world problem, and that you should just suck it up and deal with it, don't. The pervasiveness of time poverty is a serious problem, with serious costs for individuals and society. The data I and others have amassed show a correlation between time poverty and misery.[5] People who are time poor are less happy, less productive, and more stressed-out.[6] They exercise less, eat fattier food, and have a higher incidence of cardiovascular disease.[7] Time poverty forces us to compromise: instead of preparing a nutritious dinner, we grab chips and guac from the convenience store and munch mindlessly while staring at our screens. Trying to maximize our time to get things done makes our workdays a sedentary blur of salt, fat, and fast food.

Time-poor societies pay a steep price, too. The stress of being time poor costs the US health care system $190 billion, which is 5 percent to 8 percent of total health care spending each year.[8] Unhappy employees waste $450 billion–$550 billion in lost productivity each year.[9] At any given time, an organization with a thousand employees working at its offices has two hundred workers who feel so overwhelmed that they call in sick.[10]

The effects and costs of time poverty are so stark that researchers now compare it to a famine—a severe, drastic shortage of time affecting all of society—that carries many of the attendant negative consequences that a natural disaster produces.[11]

## Why Are We Time Poor?

The most obvious explanation for rising rates of time poverty is that we simply spend more time working than we used to. But evidence doesn't support this theory. Believe it or not, most people have more time for leisure now than in the 1950s.[12] In 1950, OECD data show that the average workweek in the United States was 37.8 hours; in 2017 it was 34.2. Time diaries show that in the United States, men's leisure time has increased six to nine hours per week in the past fifty years, and women's has increased four to eight hours.[13] Technology—microwaves and vacuum robots, digital communication and that snazzy feature on my email app that auto-suggests meeting times (the best!)—helps us live more-efficient lives. With the rise of the sharing economy, companies like Uber and TaskRabbit also make time-saving services more accessible and affordable.[14]

Of course, we don't have more or less time than we used to. We are all democratically afforded twenty-four hours per day. In theory, we should be happy to have gained leisure hours compared with our parents and grandparents. Why, then, do we feel more time poor than ever?

It's because time poverty doesn't necessarily arise from a mismatch between the hours we have and the hours we need. It results from how we *think about* and *value* those hours. It's as much psychological as it is structural. We might not be working more hours, but we are making decisions to work at all hours.[15] We are ceaselessly connected.[16] It's easy to continuously pay attention to that which we believe will make us more money. Valuable free time arrives; we are unprepared to use it and so we waste it. Or we tell ourselves we shouldn't take a break, so we work through it.

It's not our fault we've ended up like this. Culturally, the inherent value of time has been suppressed. Society teaches us that we should hero-worship people who never leave the office.[17] Moreover, rising income inequality makes us feel as if our world could collapse tomorrow if we don't spend every moment working, or at least appearing to work.[18] These factors create what I call *time traps*, which lead most of us to feel chronically time poor.

The first step to becoming time smart is to understand these time traps and identify them in your life.

## Time Trap 1: Technology

### Time Confetti and the Broken Promise of Leisure

It's true: we have more time for leisure than we did fifty years ago. But leisure has never been less relaxing, mostly because of the disintermediating effects of our screens. Technology saves us time, but it also takes it away. This is known as the **autonomy paradox**. We adopt mobile technologies to gain autonomy over when and how long we work, yet, ironically, we end up working all the time.[19] Long blocks of free time we used to enjoy are now interrupted constantly by our smart watches, phones, tablets, and laptops.

This situation taxes us cognitively, and fragments our leisure time in a way that makes it hard to use this time for something that will relieve stress or make us happy.[20] I (and other researchers) call this phenomenon **time confetti**, which amounts to little bits of seconds and minutes lost to unproductive multitasking.[21] Each bit alone seems not very bad. Collectively, though, all that confetti adds up to something more pernicious than you might expect.

To get a sense of how you shred your time, consider this simple calculation. You have one hour of leisure at 7 p.m. During that hour, you receive two emails, check both, and respond to one; four Twitter notifications about useless pontificating or terrible people saying terrible

TABLE 1-1

| Activity | Seconds used |
|---:|:---|
| Check 2 emails | 30 |
| Respond to 1 email | 30 |
| Check 4 Twitter notifications | 45 |
| Check replies to 1 Twitter notification | 30 |
| Check 3 Slack notifications | 30 |
| Reply to 1 Slack notification | 45 |
| Check 1 alarm reminder | 10 |
| Check 4 texts | 40 |
| Reply to 4 texts | 120 |
| **Total pieces of time confetti** | **Total time used** |
| **21** | **6m20s** |

things, and you thumb through the replies for one of them; three Slack notifications from colleagues asking you questions or a favor, of which you answer one and ignore two; one alarm reminding you to call your mother tomorrow on her birthday; and four texts from a friend trying to make plans for next weekend, all four of which you reply to.

Each event in itself is mundane and takes only seconds. But collectively they create two negative effects. The first is the sheer volume of time they take away from your hour, as shown in table 1-1.

A few seemingly harmless interruptions usurp 10 percent of this leisure time. Research shows that our estimates of the number and nature of these interruptions is conservative, so typically it may be worse than this.[22]

The second, more invasive effect of time confetti is the way it fragments the hour of leisure. It's most likely that these interruptions are randomly distributed throughout the hour. To show how, I group these interruptions into five events—email, Twitter, Slack, alarm, and texts—and randomly distribute them throughout the hour.

When we do this, that free hour turns from the image shown in figure 1-1 into something more like one of the images in figure 1-2.

FIGURE 1-1

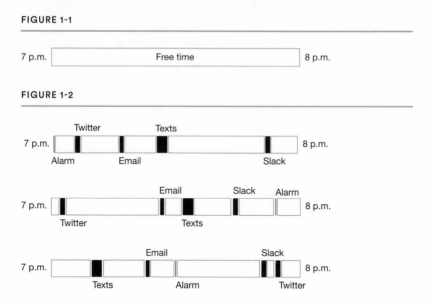

FIGURE 1-2

In each case, the hour of leisure becomes several smaller chunks, sometimes only five or six minutes long. Even if you're disciplined about not responding or not responding very quickly, the interruptions undermine the quality of those smaller, less predictable chunks of leisure time by reminding you of all the activities that you *could* or *should* be doing.[23]

We used to enjoy the gym. Now we one-handedly type out a reply to the boss while trying not to fall off the treadmill. We used to have uninterrupted family dinners. Now we have hushed phone calls over cold meals. We used to have relaxing picnics. Now we have phone meetings in "private" park-side bathroom stalls. We carry the office in our back pockets, making it difficult to disconnect. Many people have admitted to checking work email after 10 p.m. during school plays, weddings, meals, "intimate encounters," and even while their wives are in labor.[24]

When we try to enjoy a birthday dinner, notifications about our friends' tropical vacation photos make our pasta taste less delicious. When we try to choose a restaurant for our next date, the endless ocean of reviews and ratings leads us to spend more time choosing our meals than savoring them. When we try to have meaningful time off with friends and family, our alerts from work create guilt and dread over what we're not getting done.

Thinking about work while trying to relax induces panic, because feelings of time poverty are caused by how well activities fit together in our mind. If we are trying to be a committed parent while our work email goes off, we can't help thinking we should be working on our next deadline instead of being present with our child. This conflict makes us feel like a bad parent ("Why am I thinking about work while trying to hang out with my kid?") *and* a bad employee ("Am I hanging out with my kids too much? Will that promotion go to someone else?").

It also takes time to cognitively recover from shifting our minds away from the present to some other stress-inducing activity.[25] People end up enjoying their free time less and, when asked to reflect on it, estimate that they had less free time than they actually did.[26] That's how invasive the technology time trap is: time confetti makes us feel even more time impoverished than we actually are.

## Time Trap 2: Money Focus

### The Wealth Paradox and the Pitfalls of Chasing Money

Screen addiction alone hasn't caused the time famine. Another trap driving us into time poverty is the cultural obsession with work and making money. We are taught and (incorrectly) believe that money, not time, will bring greater happiness.[27] Even millionaires make this mistake. My colleagues surveyed a few thousand of the world's wealthiest people (thanks to a connection with an elite bank). They asked these one-percenters how much they would need to be "perfectly happy." Three-quarters of them—even those with more than $10 million in the bank—said they would need "a lot more" to be perfectly happy ($5 million to $10 million more "at least").[28] It doesn't take a PhD in psychology to see that this mindset is probably misguided.

We've all heard the saying, "Money doesn't buy happiness," and, empirically, it's true. Research shows that money protects against sadness but doesn't buy joy.[29] Once we make enough money to pay our bills, save for the future, and have at least some fun on the weekend, making more does little for our happiness. In data from 1.7 million people in 165 countries, researchers figured out the exact dollar amount at which added money no longer increases happiness. After we make USD$65,000 per year ($60,000 globally), money stops predicting how much we laugh or smile each day. After we make USD$105,000 per year ($95,000 globally), money stops predicting how well we think we are doing in life. If anything, once people make a lot of money ($105,000 per year in the United States), they start thinking they are doing *worse* in life.[30] When we become rich, we begin to compare our lives to people even richer than we are. We chase an idea we'll never reach, because as our wealth increases, so does our sense that others are doing better than we are and that we need to, *we can*, catch them.[31]

Money isn't all bad. Having more of it shields us from stress. When your car breaks down, money provides a solution. Having cash on hand even provides peace of mind in the absence of a crisis.[32] But staving off negative outcomes is different from creating happier ones. I will repeat this point, because it's so important: money does not buy joy. We believe that money is a path to time affluence and happiness. But we're wrong.[33] If anything, wealthier people are more stressed.[34] Instead, true happiness demands an investment of our time.

Although most of us are time poor, the (working) wealthy feel *more* time poor.[35] This makes sense in part because their higher wages mean that, literally, their time is more valuable than those who earn less (each hour worked earns them more money). The increased value of time makes it feel more precious and scarce. To demonstrate this, my colleagues turned college students into professional consultants, asking them to charge $1.50 or $0.15 for each minute that they spent working on a lab task. Students who charged $1.50 for their time felt more pressed for time than students who charged $0.15.[36] In another study, wealthier employees were more likely to agree with statements such as, "There have not been enough minutes in a day."[37]

As wealth increases, so do our feelings of time poverty. The problem is that a culture obsessed with making more money believes, wrongly, that the way to become more time affluent is to become financially wealthier.[38] Somehow, accruing money will allow us to buy happiness in the future: we think, *I'll work hard and make more so that I can afford more leisure time later.* This is the wrong solution; soon you'll see that it's the opposite of the right solution. Focusing on chasing wealth is a trap. It leads only to an increased focus on chasing wealth.[39]

# Time Trap 3: Undervalued Time

### The "Cheapest Cost" Culture and Misunderstanding What Time Is Worth

Because of a cultural obsession with money, many people protect their money in ways that are counterproductive to time affluence. Seeking the best deal and lowest price from a purely dollars-and-cents perspective contributes to time poverty and unhappiness, because we don't calculate the time costs of being so cash conscious.[40]

In one of my surveys, 52 percent of people who were financially comfortable but extremely time poor—working parents with young kids—said they'd rather have more money than more time.[41] Asked how they would spend a (hypothetical) $100 prize to increase their happiness, only 2 percent of working parents said they would spend this money to save time, such as by having their groceries delivered.[42] People who could clearly afford to value time—people who had an average of $3 million in the bank—still said that they would rather have more money.[43]

For most of us, the idea of trading cash for time doesn't even cross our minds. This is largely because it's hard to measure time's value.[44] Even if we're making a bad trade-off between time and money—such as driving two miles out of our way to save 10 cents per gallon on gas—it doesn't feel like a bad choice. That's because we know we have more money than if we paid more for the gas, but we don't really know the worth of the time it took.

Later, I account for such decisions, and you will be shocked to see how much value you lose by always trying to save a buck, and how time poor it's making you.

For now, you can recognize this time trap in your own life by identifying moments when you're making "cheaper" decisions. When you book a trip with connecting flights to get a slightly cheaper price, you are falling into a time trap. Suppose you save $300 on that flight, but it takes four hours out of your vacation time on each end of your trip and increases your fatigue and stress resulting from getting up early and switching planes. Would you pay $300 for an extra eight hours of vacation—a full workday's worth—along with less stress and fatigue?

My colleagues and I often struggle over whether to pay for an extra night at a hotel or fly red-eye back home after a conference to save a little money. I recently endured a red-eye flight, arrived home cranky, and entered into an awful fight with my partner. In retrospect, I'd have paid the $130 it cost to stay the extra night to salvage the day we both lost to anger and stress.

The trap is simple: we reflexively go for the lowest cost when we shouldn't. Let's look at the gas example more closely. You consistently choose to drive an extra six minutes to a different station to save 15 cents per gallon. You have a fifteen-gallon fill-up four times a month. Impulsively it seems worth it. Six minutes isn't that much, and the savings will add up. Someone aware of time traps would see it differently:

15 cents × 15 gallons = $2.25 saved per trip

$2.25 × 4 visits per month = $9.00 saved per month

$9.00 per month over 12 months = $108 saved per year

---

6 minutes per trip × 4 visits per month = 24 minutes lost per month

24 minutes per month × 12 months = 4.8 hours lost per year

Looking at it this way, you've spent almost five hours to save $108. In this case, your time is worth about $22 per hour, and that doesn't take into account the opportunity cost of what you could have done with that five hours instead of driving farther to save a little.

It's not that these calculations will always tell you to go with the more expensive option. And you may still feel that the trade-off is worth it. But doing these calculations in the moment puts a different lens on time value, which we tend to grossly underestimate.

## Time Trap 4: Busyness as Status

### The Link between Financial Uncertainty and Workism

More than ever, our identities are tied to work. The best data show that people living in the United States increasingly look toward work—not friends, families, or hobbies—to find purpose.

The idea of work as a central source of meaning has been around for several decades, but the idea of what popular press articles call "workism" is a recent and intensifying phenomenon. As Derek Thompson, a staff writer at the *Atlantic*, described it, **workism** is the "newest religion competing for congregants."[45]

Work was once more generally considered a means to an end and not an end in itself. Work to live. Now many people live to work. In a 2017 survey, 95 percent of young adults said that having an "enjoyable and meaningful career" was "extremely important" to them.[46]

I marvel at how differently students approach college since I was in their position. It was common for my friends and me to make career decisions spontaneously, pursuing whatever we found interesting at the time. In my junior year, I was a theater major, and I legitimately spent more time dressing up as Kermit the Frog than practicing linear algebra. Now students come to me in anxious droves to ask about career trajectories and internship offers in hopes of choosing the *absolute best*, *absolutely correct* career path. One student met with me five times in one semester to try to figure out her future plans. I said to her, "You are twenty years old and almost a Harvard College graduate. There are no bad choices. I spent my junior year in college dressing up in a frog costume and doing yoga for course credit, and everything turned out fine!" Let's just say she was not impressed.

Given the importance that we place on work, busyness at work now carries status. We wear it like a badge of honor.[47] We want to be seen as the employee who works the longest hours (even when these hours aren't productive). A colleague, Peter, told me that he used to stay at the office until 7 p.m.—even when he wasn't working—just so that the HR system would record his physical presence. Peter was paid a salary, so there was no direct incentive for him to work past 5 p.m. The Peters of the world make proud proclamations on social media about working nonstop and cancel social plans due to being *crazy busy*.

Financial insecurity also drives workism, and it's on the rise. Since the early 1970s, income inequality has risen dramatically in the United States and around the world.[48] As society becomes more unequal, people feel increasingly insecure about their financial future, regardless of their current stature.[49] Those doing well worry about how far they could fall. Those struggling to make ends meet fear falling farther behind. Most of us cope by working more and trying to make more money.[50] By default, we deprioritize positive time for ourselves and our friends and family; it's the easiest thing to sacrifice, because we're not sure how to measure its value anyway. We voluntarily give up vacation time lest people perceive us as not working hard.[51] We feel guilty about spending money on things that make us happy, such as dining out or vacations.[52]

This fear is deep seated, sometimes resulting from exposure to inequality at a young age. When my colleagues and I asked people how unequal their neighborhood was where they grew up, and how important money is to them right now, we discovered that people exposed to greater income inequality as kids were more likely to say their self-esteem was influenced by how much money they made.[53] It didn't matter where they lived or how much money they had in the present; financial uncertainty growing up led to a higher chronic focus on money as adults.

With our self-identity so wrapped up in work and productivity, the social appearance of being busy makes us feel good about ourselves.[54] Being busy makes us feel that we are committed as well as essential. Our hard work (or the appearance of it) could help us earn more and keep us on the perfect career track we've planned for since college. In contrast, focusing our attention on something other than work could threaten our livelihood and status. We worry we won't be valued, and, in part, we are right. Turns out employers are (mostly) rewarding the busyness cult. Research shows that employees who boast about working nonstop and being extremely busy are seen by others as better workers who have more money and prestige, even if they don't. They're even thought to be more physically attractive.[55]

Even if it feels good in the moment for someone to see the email you sent on Saturday at 8:30 p.m., this behavior contributes to an overall unhealthy and unhappy life. The workism time trap is contributing to your time poverty (and the time poverty of your colleagues).

## Time Trap 5: Idleness Aversion

### Mindfulness and the Value of Doing Nothing

Even if we lived in a perfectly equal society, we would still create time stress for ourselves: human beings are not built for idleness. Philosopher Blaise Pascal said, "All of humanity's problems stem from [our] inability to sit quietly in a room alone."

Researchers call this **idleness aversion**, and it makes us do some strange things. Dan Gilbert, a professor of psychology at Harvard, placed some college students in an empty room and gave them nothing to do. Most students, accustomed to constant stimulation and easy access to distractors, did not like this one bit.[56] Many preferred to *give themselves mild electric shocks* to being left alone with their thoughts.

As Gilbert summarized, "Most people boiled over in rage at the idea of doing nothing."[57] Lest you chalk this up to college kids being college kids, another study showed that working parents felt "bored" and "stressed" during leisure activities—signaling that even the most time poor among us don't know how to relax.[58]

Technology may help us avoid being alone with our thoughts, but it is a trap that contributes to stress and time poverty. Constant connection to technology prevents the brain from recovering, keeps our stress levels elevated, and takes us out of the present.

In fact, idleness has been shown to be a valuable form of leisure and can increase time affluence. The mindfulness movement, whether in the form of meditation, prayer, or some other framework, is effectively practiced idleness. Although mindfulness training can be completed at home and self-guided through websites and apps, it does take effort. But it's worth it. The physical and mental benefits of disengaging the brain are far more valuable than the stress created by keeping the mind engaged at all times.[59]

## Time Trap 6: The "Yes . . . Damn!" Effect

### Commitment and the False Promise of Tomorrow

Most of us are overoptimistic about our future time.[60] We believe, dumbly, that we will have more time tomorrow than we do today.[61] This is sometimes referred to as the **planning fallacy**.[62] I call it the **"Yes . . . damn!"** effect. Let me explain.

Last Monday, over coffee, a friend asked me if I could help her move on Saturday. No problem. On Tuesday, a colleague asked me to look over her report by Saturday. I said yes. On Wednesday, another friend invited me out for dinner on Saturday at a new restaurant that I wanted to try. As a happiness researcher, I know that socializing is good for me, so I said yes.

You see what's happening. I said yes over and over (and over), until Saturday morning, when I woke up and thought, *Damn! What was I thinking?*

Actually, as a researcher, I know what I was thinking: *Even though I'm too busy now, Saturday is a ways off, and I'll have time to do these things.* The cost of saying yes in the present is low (and it feels good to say yes to people), and the future seems like a place filled with open time—that is, until the future becomes the present, and we often wish we could take back the things we said yes to.

Statistically, the best predictor of how busy we are going to be next week is how busy we are right now. So the decision to say yes to later commitments even though I'm too busy now is a bad bet. Our minds frequently forget this important point and trick us into believing we'll have more time later than we do now. This overoptimism means that we're cavalier with our yeses, even for small stuff we don't want to do (you'll learn more about how to say no in chapter 4). We genuinely want to say yes to everything we get asked to do. We see saying yes as a way to overcome idleness and feel productive, connected, valued, respected, and loved.

And where does the time to fulfill these commitments come from? From the leisure time that we could be using to feel more time affluent, of course. We run ourselves around from activity to activity, feeling pressed for time, failing to enjoy ourselves. We keep ourselves overwhelmed in the hopes that this busyness will provide us fulfillment.[63] Ironically, perpetual busyness undermines the goals that we set out to achieve with all our busyness in the first place.[64]

## Overcoming Time Traps

These six time traps are the most common; I suspect you can relate to at least a few. There are many more reasons that we fail to prioritize time, such as the fear of judgment from other people and several others that I share in more detail later.

For now, your goal should be to recognize and document the time traps that you fall into most often. They won't be the same as other people's. What makes it a trap for you is that it makes you unhappy and steals time that you would otherwise use in a way that makes you happy. The toolkit at the end of this chapter is designed to help you think about and internalize the traps you are most vulnerable to so that in the coming chapters you can form strategies to overcome them.

We all have the power to overcome the time traps we have fallen victim to. As with efforts to get fit, increasing your time affluence requires taking small, deliberate steps each day to enjoy your free time (and have more of it). And like getting fit, it's not easy at first. Both society and our psychology conspire against us to make the traps extremely appealing.

I am an expert on this topic. I spend most of my days writing, talking about, and researching the importance of having free time—and I am still somewhat time poor. I struggle to protect my free time as much as I should. The one time that I was spotted enjoying myself on vacation my friend posted a photo of me on social media with the caption, "Proof you sometimes do stuff outside of the office!" This post was my most "liked" last year (groan).

Keeping the exercise metaphor going, just as you shouldn't punish yourself for not being perfect in your workout habits, don't ever beat yourself up about being bad at prioritizing time. Remember, multiple forces are making it difficult. We don't naturally respond to time poverty in a way that controls it. Actually, when we feel busy, studies show that we start taking on *more* tasks. A roommate of mine during final exams in college was so anxious about studying for tests that he decided to take on more shifts at work and obsessively run errands. He cooked and concocted new protein shake recipes, usurping time he could have used to study and reinforcing the cycle. Stress spurs busyness, which creates stress, which spurs busyness.

A friend pointed out that this behavior is the diet equivalent of saying, "Wow, I feel fat—time to have another burger." In contrast to this example, there's an absurd logic at play here. When we feel time poor, we take on small, easy-to-complete tasks because they help us feel more control over our time.[65] We think, *There! I made a protein shake and finished that errand. I'm getting stuff done!* In this case, it's a false sense of control that doesn't alleviate the root cause of our busyness.

Time poverty feels the same for everyone, but time affluence looks different for everyone. It could mean spending fifteen more minutes strumming the guitar instead of scrolling through your phone, or it could be ten minutes of meditation, or a Saturday morning learning how to invest your savings instead of Slacking about work gossip. No matter what time affluence looks like for you, the happiest and most time affluent among us are deliberate with their free time. Working toward time affluence is about recognizing and overcoming the time traps in our lives and intentionally carving out happier and more meaningful moments each day.

Use the toolkit exercises on the following pages to get a better sense of the time traps that you fall into. In chapter 2, you will build on these reflections by further scrutinizing your time use and devising personal strategies for creating time affluence and happier ways to spend your time.

## *chapter 1 toolkit*

The following tools will help you diagnose your degree of time poverty and the time traps you fall into.

### The Six Common Time Traps

- **Constant connection to technology.** Cell phones, laptops, and other technology constantly interrupt us, fragment work and leisure into confetti, and create stress.

- **Obsession with work and making money.** People incorrectly believe that money, not time, will bring greater happiness, and that if they work and make money now, they will have more time to relax in the future. In reality, making money only leads to an increased interest in chasing wealth.

- **Limited value placed on time.** People do not correctly value their time. They often give up large amounts of time to save very little money.

- **Busyness as a status symbol.** People look to work to find meaning, and they use busyness at work to help shape their identity and self-worth.

- **Aversion to idleness.** People don't see the value in disconnecting, even though there is proven value to being mindful, enjoying the present, and doing nothing.

- **The Yes . . . damn! effect.** People are overly optimistic about their future time. They think they will have more time tomorrow than they do today. This overoptimism means they say yes to many requests for their future time and then regret it ("damn!") when that time comes and they are overcommitted.

## Time Poverty Diagnostic Tools

Thinking about your life overall, how much spare time do you have? Use a scale of −5 to 5, where −5 is *very little* or *no spare time*, and 5 is *lots of spare time.*

Record your answer here: _____

Thinking about your life overall, how much spare money do you have? Use a scale of −5 to 5, where −5 is *very little* or *no spare money*, and 5 is *lots of spare money.*

Record your answer here: _____

Now plot your answers on this grid:

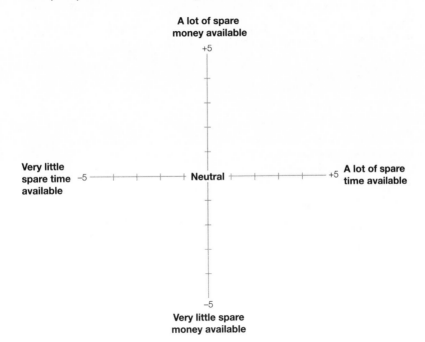

If your score is in the lower left, you are **extremely** time poor. You might be more likely to value money over time, contributing to your time poverty. If your score is in the upper left, you are **typically** time poor. You feel that you don't have very much time available but might still have a time-centric mindset. If your score is on the right side of the grid, you are likely **not very** time poor because you report having spare time available.

Everyone benefits from putting time first, but you might want to spend more energy and attention alleviating time poverty if you are **extremely** or **typically** time poor.

# Evaluate Yourself

Think about your own decisions about time and money, and the time traps that you fall into.

In the table below, document which time traps affect you most, and describe the specific decisions that you make in each category. For example, in the technology time trap, you might write, "Spend too much time researching small purchases."

| Time trap | Your time trap habit |
| --- | --- |
| **Technology** (checking texts, emails, and other notifications; using websites to research decisions, etc.) | |
| **Work obsession** (focusing on earning more money in hopes you'll reach a point where you're satisfied, and it will free up time then) | |
| **Undervalued time** (choosing the cheapest price no matter how much time it costs) | |
| **Busyness as status** (appearing to be working at all times and tying self-worth to work) | |
| **Idleness aversion** (fearing that downtime is wasted time and filling it with low-value activities) | |
| **The Yes . . . damn! effect** (committing to too many future activities because it seems you'll have more time in the future) | |

# 2

## *steps to finding time and funding time*

So far, you've reflected on your feelings of time poverty, documented a few ways in which you fall into the six most common time traps, and determined whether you broadly value time or money.

Now it's time to get specific. We face thousands, maybe tens of thousands of these time–money decisions each year. Some, such as career decisions, take time and carry profound consequences.[1] Other decisions are made in seconds, such as deciding whether to take an Uber or a commuter train to the airport.[2] A few barely register in our consciousness, such as turning to our phone when it buzzes.

Before I started studying time–money trade-offs, I often overlooked small, potentially costly decisions. I thought about time and money when I made big decisions, but I never stopped to think about these trade-offs as I went about my daily life. Now I can't choose a coffee shop or plan a road trip without considering how long I might have to wait in line or whether there is a toll bridge that I could take to get somewhere faster.

Getting into the habit of being mindful is a good first step, but to significantly improve your time affluence you need a plan, along with strategies to help you make decisions.

Here's that plan.

## Step 1: Know Your Default Setting

You've already started this step by identifying with Taylor or Morgan (in the introduction). Recall that each character represents an extreme version of a person who either values time over money (Taylor) or who values money over time (Morgan). Now let's add a sense of *how much* of a Taylor or a Morgan you are.

At one extreme is a Morgan I've come to know in the course of my research. He works in medicine and structures his life around making money and being productive. In his words, "When I'm at home, I'm unhappy because I'm not making money, so I'd rather be at work." He works a full shift at the hospital and volunteers to be on call at night. To be closer to work, he lives in a different apartment from his pregnant wife. He hasn't fully furnished this apartment because "that would cost money." He has instructed his wife to text him "exactly one hour" before she is set to deliver their baby so that he can leave work, say hello to the new addition to the family, and make it back to the hospital where he works in time to finish his shift.

You might wonder what the rest of his life is like. Honestly, he doesn't have much of one. He doesn't exercise; he eats dinner in his car or at the hospital cafeteria almost every day; he's overweight. To be clear: I am not making up this Morgan. He is a real person. You may have tagged yourself as a Morgan, but not *that much* of one.

I've met extreme Taylors, too, including a digital media strategist who would rather buy a significantly more expensive toaster quickly than spend hours of his life researching the best deal. "Why would I waste my time with that?" He lives in the city, where his rent is ex-

FIGURE 2-1

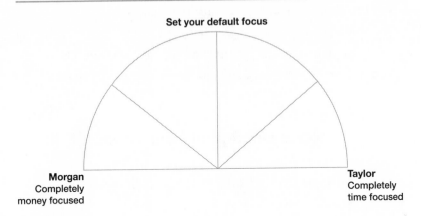

**Set your default focus**

**Morgan**
Completely
money focused

**Taylor**
Completely
time focused

pensive, but he can walk or bike to work (so he doesn't own a car or spend time stuck in traffic). He'll welcome a promotion but isn't willing to "sacrifice weekends or vacation" for one. He never checks email outside office hours. He doesn't own a TV. His "dumb phone" can't connect to the internet, and he shuts it off at night. He rarely makes plans. Instead, he "lets [his] friends haggle over where they're going, what they're doing, where they're eating, when they're meeting" and then "just shows up."

Perhaps you think of yourself as a Taylor but not to that extent. You like Netflix and have been known to work after 5 p.m. or check email on Sunday evening.

Most of us fall between these two examples. Think about how close to the extremes you are, and then mark on the spectrum in figure 2-1 where you see yourself.

Remember, these default mindsets aren't good or bad; they're set through our life experiences and social environments. People who grew up poor, live in areas with high levels of income inequality, and feel uncertain about their financial future learn to focus more on work and making money.[3] And this is likely the right decision. People who are struggling to make ends meet are often happier when their default is set on the money side of the spectrum.[4]

Yet people who value money, and are in a position to be happier that way, still benefit from making time-related choices. The years of data I've collected suggest that no matter where you start, you should move at least a little bit toward the Taylor (time) side of the spectrum. The people who accumulate time affluence and happiness have done just that.[5]

## Step 2: Document Your Time

To start increasing your time affluence, you need a baseline under-standing of your time-use decisions. One of the best ways to do this is to spend an upcoming Tuesday keeping a detailed log of how you spend your time. (You'll find one in the toolkit at the end of this chapter.)

Why Tuesday? Tuesdays tend to be fairly routine workdays when people usually experience more negative feelings and greater stress than other days, so it will capture more of the activities that are making you time poor.[6] If you can't do a Tuesday, pick another work weekday.[7]

Note exactly how you feel about each activity beyond positive or neg-ative. For example, was the activity unproductive or productive? Pleas-urable or purposeful? This additional step is important when you're accounting for your time and thinking about the *meaning* that certain activities add to your life.[8]

Parenting, for example, comes with a lot of tension and, after the sixteenth consecutive sleepless night, not a lot of pleasure. Yet for most people, nothing is more rewarding than watching their toddler take their first steps.[9] Becoming a human taco on the couch while watching your favorite TV show is highly enjoyable, although it is not exactly a source of existential meaning. We should pay extra attention to time spent in unproductive activities that make us stressed, and we should ask ourselves whether we can focus more on accumulating productive, pleasurable, or meaningful experiences instead.[10]

Once you've documented your activities, reflect on them. Think about which activities were pleasurable versus painful; which were productive versus unproductive; and which brought you pleasure versus meaning. For activities that made you stressed and unhappy, ask yourself whether it's possible to spend less time on them. For any task you can't (or shouldn't) get out of—like work or exercise—ask yourself whether it is possible to make the activity more pleasant or less tense.

## Step 3: Find Time

Being stuck in tasks we don't like and can't control is one of the leading causes of time poverty.[11] As a result, the easiest and most obvious path to greater time affluence is to deliberately choose to spend more time on activities that bring you joy, and less time on activities that bring you misery.[12] For fans of minimalism, this approach can be thought of as the Marie Kondo method of time use, after the famous organizer of people's homes and lives.

Adapting her framework for our purpose looks something like this:

- Observe how you spend your time.

- Ask yourself, *Do I love this activity or not?*

- If not, get rid of it.

For fans of labor economics, this approach can be thought of as maximizing your personal u-Index:[13]

- Calculate the percentage of time you spend in activities that bring you happiness versus those that give you misery.

- Maximize the positive.

- Minimize the negative.

In any case, you're **finding time** to transform daily activities from the kind that make you feel time poor to the kind that make you feel time affluent. There are several ways to find time.

## Transform Bad Time

Finding time starts with taking small moments of "bad" time—while commuting or waiting in line—and injecting it with happiness-producing activities such as listening to audiobooks or music.

Without much effort you can probably think of several activities that you can transform. Meetings are a source of time poverty for many people, so review your calendar and uninvite yourself from as many meetings as possible, and use that time to walk outside instead. Close email until the end of the day so you aren't constantly bombarded by interruptions. Turn off your cell phone on Saturday, and enjoy making and eating grilled cheese sandwiches with your niece.

In practice this will look different for everyone, because we all love and loathe different things. Some find a trip to the museum unsatisfying, while others return again and again. The key is to identify the time *you* don't like and look for ways to transform it.

Committing to only one of these simple strategies can alter your time affluence, and you should calculate the time shift to see how. Suppose you find time to practice guitar instead of attending an optional forty-five-minute meeting that takes place on Fridays, when you typically work from home. The simple calculation of forty-five minutes over fifty-two weeks means you've transformed thirty-nine hours—a day and a half—of your year. And the added benefit of using these thirty-nine hours for something that brings you joy can intensify the time affluence effect.

## Augment Good Time

You can also find time by adding to your positive experiences. Is there a positive activity (either productive or unproductive) that you want to do more of? For me, reading and listening to music are two of my happiest experiences, so I am purposeful about filling my downtime with those activities.

Even a few minutes of your happiest or most purposeful activities can make a difference. One night a week, you might order takeout and spend the time reading instead.

## Hack Work Time

Almost everything about having a job is conspiring to make us time poor: the time spent getting ready for work; the commute; unhealthy eating squeezed into our day (or not eating at all because we're too busy); the after-work decompression. These negative, time-poor activities feed on themselves: if we feel time pressed, we're less deliberate about seizing our free time.[14] In our brief moments of downtime, we engage in time-poor activities such as looking at our phones. Time-poor people who feel overwhelmed at work spend more money than time-affluent people on material purchases that distract but don't provide happiness or meaning.[15]

Coordinating with your boss to work from home one day every other week would immediately eliminate 10 percent of these kinds of time-impoverishing activities. Working from home once a week cuts one-fifth of the misery. Even if you have to work your regular hours, you will not suffer from the stress created on either end of the day, and research suggests you will be more productive and healthier in those hours.[16] Ask your boss for a bit of flextime. Tell them I sent you. If it's not possible to work from home, take all your breaks and all your paid vacation so that you can press Reset and come back to work refreshed.[17]

## Practice the Right Kind of Leisure Time

It's important we do not spend all of our free time flipping through internet memes and generally lying about. Free time devoted to **active leisure**—activities like volunteering, socializing, and exercising—promotes happiness far more than spending time engaged in **passive leisure** activities like watching TV, napping, or online shopping.[18]

Even simply moving your body helps: research shows that those who've moved within the past twenty-five minutes report higher happiness.[19]

When my colleagues and I studied this, we were not surprised to see that millionaires were (a tiny bit) happier than people with minimal wealth. Although having more money doesn't predict joy, it can predict life satisfaction, which is what we measured in this study. However, money wasn't what made these millionaires happier. Controlling for wealth, the millionaires spent thirty more minutes per day engaged in active leisure, and forty fewer minutes engaged in passive leisure like "watching TV" or "doing nothing." That's a seventy-minute swing in time-affluent behavior.[20] Over a year, this practice creates a large gap in time use, with the wealthy devoting hundreds more hours to activities that make them feel more time affluent and happier.

## Find More Time for Meals

Along with my Parisian (naturally) colleague Romain Cadario, I discovered in a survey of more than ten thousand people that the French spend more time each day eating, while Americans spend more time choosing what they are going to eat than enjoying their meals.[21] Because of their focus on savoring, the French derived greater satisfaction from eating, making them feel less stressed. There's time to be found in all the before-meal activity of choosing a place, getting there, choosing from the menu, and getting on with our day. Eating out seems to be a classic happiness-inducing activity, but it may be less effective at combating stress than simply ordering delivery (or even better, auto-ordering something you've ordered in the past) and then sitting back and enjoying your meal and the company.[22]

## Find Time to Meet New People and Help Others

The benefits of having high-quality social connections are similar to those of getting regular exercise and not smoking.[23] Even fleeting social interactions with strangers—like chatting with the person sitting next to you on a flight—improves mood.[24]

The social interaction of volunteering not only makes us happy but also helps us feel less time poor. In one study, researchers asked people to spend between ten and thirty minutes doing something for themselves that they weren't already planning to do, or to spend time doing something for someone else that they weren't already planning to do. When people spent additional time helping someone else, they felt that their future was less limited.

This may seem backward, because volunteering actually takes time. But this prosocial activity boosts mood and increases time affluence, because we feel more in control of our time when we feel we can choose to give some of it away.[25] If you commit to finding two minutes per day to say hi to a stranger or do something for someone else, you'll have added twelve hours of prosocial time to your year.

## Find Time to Experience Awe

Taking scenic hikes or spending a few moments looking up into the sky can rejuvenate you. Awe-inspiring experiences reduce time stress.[26] When you're thinking about what activities to add to your schedule, try blocking in time for a walk in the park—being surrounded by nature— or watching a scenic YouTube video at your desk.[27]

• • •

Even if you feel time poor, the moments are there to recapture. The list of daily activities you make for yourself in this chapter's toolkit, along with the process of pinpointing the activities that are ripe for removal and replacement, is the best place to start increasing your time affluence.

# Step 4: Fund Time

You can find time largely for free. It costs no money to cancel one optional meeting a week and take a walk instead. But there is a more direct way to subtract negative, time-impoverishing experiences, and that's to buy your way out. You can fund time.

The startup community uses this tactic well. Venture capitalists (VCs) advise mentees to outsource as much work as possible that isn't core to their entrepreneurial idea. This practice lets them focus only on their most mission-critical work. They hire chefs so that they don't have to spend time on meals; they buy into workspaces close to or even in the same building as collaborators to cut down on travel; they buy high-end conferencing and collaboration software to make remote work as effective and efficient as possible. (Whether or not this obsession with work is, overall, creating time poverty is another matter, but the principle of funding time is identical to what you'll be doing.) They are onto something: we know, for example, that CEOs who use meal-prep services and delegate tasks to senior leadership generally feel better about their time use.[28]

Wealthy CEOs don't have to be the only beneficiaries. Funding time is effective—more effective than you think—regardless of where you live, your age, your gender (men and women benefit equally), how much you work, or how much money you make. It takes less money than you may suspect to increase time affluence, and you should spend more than you suspect to reap the benefits.

In one experiment, I provided working adults with two payments of $40. On one weekend I asked participants to spend this $40 on a material purchase, and they bought stuff for themselves such as t-shirts, board games, and makeup. On the next weekend, I asked participants to spend the $40 in "any way that would save time," and they ordered takeout, took taxis instead of the bus, and had their groceries delivered. The time-saving purchases made them feel happier and less stressed.[29]

To decide whether outsourcing is worth it to you, ask yourself whether your time is worth more than what it would cost to outsource some of your most negative and unproductive experiences.[30] When I looked at the activities on my list, the miserable time stuck in traffic on my way to work was the time I most wanted back. So I checked what it would cost to take an Uber from my house to work and then use that time to read and listen to (and discover new) music—activities I enjoy immensely.

I invested to convert a time-poor activity (commuting) into a time-affluent activity (reading and expanding my musical tastes). I also paid money for a music subscription service to eliminate ads from my music listening.

That may seem extravagant, but let's compute it.

**Costs:**

> Ride share @ $30/day, 20 days/month = $600
>
> Streaming service @ $12/month = $12
>
> Total cost: $612 / month

**Benefits:**

> Time gained back: 45 minutes/day, 20 days/month = 15 hours
>
> Commute stress reduced to near zero
>
> Approximately 165 more hours per year of pleasurable and meaningful activities

I've gained back nearly two workdays each month that previously were filled with stress that carried into my day. And I redeployed that time to activities that contribute to my time affluence and happiness, all for about $600 per month, or $40 per hour. I consider that a good deal. Remember, it's not a new expense. I incur a $600 cost, but I am no longer paying for a car lease, gas, or parking, which had cost me $500 per month. Another way to frame this decision is that I've spent an extra $100 to gain back fifteen hours per month. For me, the comparative advantage of taking an Uber outweighed the cost savings of driving.

You may still pause. It seems like a lot of money, and culturally it feels like an extravagance. If you feel you can't afford to outsource an entire task, think about removing your most disliked tasks half the time, or a quarter of the time, or when your schedule is especially tense and busy. My research shows that this is when funding time pays off most.[31]

Also, don't underestimate how much it's worth spending to get your time back. It seems like a lot, because you've been hardwired to always think about spending as little money as possible. Moreover, it's hard to know how much money these hard-to-quantify ideas, such as experiencing less stress and gaining time doing something you love, are worth. Soon you'll calculate the value of such factors. In the meantime, you might be surprised by how much better you'll feel spending extra money for what might seem like an extravagance.

And you can look for material purchases (that likely are not making you as happy as you think) that you can remove to supplement your funding of time. I "found" $100 to contribute to my ride share by getting rid of my daily coffee-shop purchases and refraining from unnecessary online orders.

Now let's look at other strategies to think about when you're funding time.

## Subtract Your Chores, but Not Too Many

If you're stuck trying to figure out exactly how to outsource your chores, companies like Angie's List, Beyond the Rack, and TaskRabbit make it possible, and more affordable than ever, to fund time. Spending on time-saving services—like shopping, cleaning, and laundry—can reduce time stress and increase happiness. But buyer beware: outsourcing too much becomes a management job that brings stress. Suddenly, your schedule is out of control and you're juggling setting up and managing appointments, deliveries, and so on.[32]

## Understand What You Want to Outsource

Don't assume that because making dinner is stressful, you should just order food. Research I conducted with the smart phone application Joy showed that many consumers were more satisfied with subscription dinner services than food delivery.[33] This is probably because many of us like cooking, but we don't like having to think about what we're going to make or how to purchase ingredients in the right amount.

So think critically about your disliked tasks. What is it you really don't like? Do you not like commuting, or is it that you usually don't do anything else except stare at someone else's bumper during that time instead of paying to stream music or a podcast? Look to fund the most disliked part of the task you don't like doing.

For example, funding time by using a grocery delivery service allows you to spend more minutes engaged in the part of making a meal that you like—cooking. Again, a quick calculation shows you're still saving time: getting rid of deciding what to eat (ten minutes) and shopping for the food (twenty minutes) only once a week frees up twenty-six hours in a year. You might save more time ordering takeout, but you'd also remove positive cooking time.

One person in my study got this down.[34] When documenting tasks that she wanted to fund, she was careful to distinguish between chores in general and the kinds of chores specifically that made her miserable. She said, "I am neurotic, so doing laundry and dishes and de-cluttering the house makes me feel like I am putting my life in order. Spending twenty or thirty minutes a day tidying up puts me in a good mood and makes me feel like I am in control. In contrast, 'deep cleaning,' like washing baseboards, scrubbing toilets, mopping the floor, and sweeping the porch, makes me miserable. The thought of these chores makes me unhappy, and it also makes me resent my husband because he avoids the entire situation. So I hire someone once per month to do these things."

## Don't Assume You Can't Afford to Fund Time

Even those on strict budgets can fund time and should spend more than they may suspect doing it.[35]

Take Cameron, an undergraduate student. After listening to me talk about the importance of focusing on time over money, he tried to implement these strategies even though he was a poorly paid student. He gleefully recounted his efforts to me: "Since I started my new job, I have had to start work at 6 a.m. on Saturday mornings. With my first month's pay, I bought a used bike off Craigslist, which cut my commute down considerably (I used to walk). It now only takes me six minutes to get to work! And, more recently, I bought a new coffee machine with auto-start. Now, every Saturday morning at 4:57 a.m., my coffee machine kicks in and brews hazelnut coffee! This allows me a few more valuable minutes in bed. These purchases have allowed me to cut down on the time I'm spending in the morning, reducing the pressure of being late to work. I would say that's money well spent!"

## If You Still Feel Guilty, Ask for Time Saving as a Gift

You may still feel guilty about outsourcing. *I'm not that kind of person,* you tell yourself. Even when I present evidence that it's worth it and will increase your happiness, some people can't bring themselves to try it.[36] If that's you, ask for time as a gift. Get others to fund your time if they intended to spend money on you anyway. We tend not to give these kinds of gifts, but people perceive gifts given with the intention of saving time to be more thoughtful and appreciated than gifts that are given with the intention of saving money, especially because most of us hesitate to make time-saving purchases for ourselves.[37]

As one woman explained to me, "My marriage was saved by hiring someone to do the cleaning. When we both worked full-time it was almost impossible to do everything, and the house suffered. But we felt pretty uncomfortable regularly making time-saving purchases, since we were trying to pay off our house. So, when asked what gift I wanted for my birthday or Christmas, I would always say someone to do the cleaning. Imagine my delight when one birthday that's what I received! I joke that I hate cleaning so much that if there was a hell, and I was sent there, that is what my job assignment would be. Luckily, since I was gifted time, I don't have to be trapped in my own personal hell (cleaning)."[38]

A word of warning: despite this story, time-saving gifts are more appreciated by the recipient in professional contexts rather than romantic relationships.[39] They're also more appreciated for activities the recipient doesn't enjoy.[40] Giving time gifts isn't a panacea; you also must give gifts that are based on the other person's preference.[41] Gift givers: if someone likes cooking, they are less appreciative of an automatic mixer that saves time than someone who hates making dessert.

## Do Less Comparison Shopping

The amount of time that is used to find the cheapest price is often more valuable than the amount of money that you end up saving. Driving farther for cheaper gas or going from store to store to find the same outfit at a lower price likely costs more time than it's worth.

I was thrilled to see my editor employ this strategy when buying a new TV. Normally, he's one to do deep research on such a purchase, poring over pixel densities, feature lists, and refresh rates and future-proofing his investment. He reads reviews online, and then, when he has narrowed his choices, he goes to stores to look at the TVs in person to make sure he's happy with his research; then he goes store-to-store to find the one with the best price. The process takes hours and can take up most of a weekend, if not more.

This time, though, he set a price range, looked at reviews for a few TVs in that range, and picked one. That's it. The whole process took less than thirty minutes. "It was really hard for me at first to get out of that mindset that I have to get the best TV for the best price," he said. "But in the end, say I paid an extra hundred dollars. So what? I got my whole weekend back. Probably fifteen hours at least, for major purchases. It has really changed how I think about shopping."

## Step 5: Reframe Time

We can count up minutes and assign costs to our time, and we should. But we can also change how we *feel* about our time, and that can make us more time affluent, too.

For example, we know from research that deliberately savoring an experience can change our perception of it.[42] In one study, the simple instruction to treat the upcoming weekend "like a holiday" changed how people approached their weekends by increasing how much they savored their free time, improving their mood.[43] Conversely, ruminating on the past (e.g., thinking about our workweek) or anticipating the future (e.g., thinking about our upcoming week) makes us feel pressed for time. By focusing our attention in the present, we become sensitive to existing pleasures, increasing time affluence in the process.[44]

Even the most time-destroying thing of all, our jobs, can be reframed. If you work in a physically demanding job like construction or retail where you're on your feet all day, you can reframe this activity. Research shows that when people think about these physical demands as "exercise," they like their jobs more and feel more physically fit.[45] In one study, a group of hotel room attendants were told that the activity they did at work met their recommended levels of activity to be an active and healthy person. This simple shift also resulted in significant reductions in weight, body fat, and blood pressure among those workers.[46]

Similarly, people who deliberately set goals during their car commute, such as planning for their upcoming day, enjoyed their commute more and were less likely to want to quit their jobs, because they felt more prepared for the day ahead.[47] These studies suggest that you can find better time by reframing what you think is bad time as some form of good time.

### Meta-Reframing: The Time Value of Valuing Time

One of the most valuable ways to gain time affluence is to recognize the value of time affluence.[48] Taking moments to acknowledge the preciousness of time changes how we feel about it and encourages us to extract more happiness from even the most mundane activities.[49]

Research repeatedly demonstrates this phenomenon. When told to imagine that it was their last month in the city where they lived, people suddenly gained greater satisfaction from time that otherwise went by unnoticed and undervalued, such as walking through a park, noticing art, and seeing pets and people.[50] When researchers asked people to give up something they loved for seven days (chocolate, of course), they savored it more the next time they tasted it.[51]

Research I'm doing on near-death experiences gives us some of the best findings on the time value of valuing time.[52] I've discovered that people who've nearly died feel as if time moves more slowly. They are more grateful for daily experiences, and they prioritize socially focused goals over professionally productive ones. As one person who died (four times!) on the operating table explained to me, "Every single one of my relationships has changed. I have a new respect for the people I love and take nothing for granted. My mother and I are much closer. My sisters and I are much closer. It has made me see how short life really is!"

A harrowing experience was foisted on this person, but you don't need to nearly die to start gaining time affluence. In fact, you've already started. The act of accounting for your time and writing down how long you're spending on tasks is cultivating an appreciation for time.[53] Even reading this book is a good first step toward cultivating a greater appreciation for time and greater time affluence.[54]

● ● ●

I'm often asked, "How much time should I spend finding time versus funding time?" There's no one answer. Start by looking back at the Taylor or Morgan spectrum. If you are a moderate to deeply devoted Morgan and are money-focused (like me), you'll likely want to spend more effort finding time versus funding time. Trying too hard to fund time will likely cause you stress.[55] So any funding you do should be strategic and low risk. In contrast, if you skew toward Taylor, focus on funding time. You won't worry as much about spending cash to buy back time. But you should also spend some effort on finding time as well.[56]

No matter what you value, make sure that you leave enough time for active leisure activities like socializing, vacations, hobbies, and volunteering. And, of course, try to reframe your time. All of these activities reduce stress, whether you value money or time.

So far, this chapter has been focused on forming the building blocks of new habits. Even after reading this far you still might be skeptical about putting time first, because it's harder to trust the value of time gained versus money saved. Money is easy to measure, whereas smarter time is harder to gauge. We need a metric to show us how much our time is worth. The following section provides a framework for starting.

## Account for Your Time

Here's a dilemma: after you put in five hours of work for a colleague, they give you two tickets to see your favorite band. A few days before, you put in fifteen hours of work for another colleague, who gave you two tickets to see another decent concert on the same night. Both shows would make for a good night's entertainment, but the first band is your favorite and you'd prefer that one. Which do you go to?[57]

**Option A:** Favorite band, reward for 5 hours of work

**Option B:** Good band, reward for 15 hours of work

Now imagine that you were forced to make the same decision, but instead of getting the tickets in exchange for time you put in at work, you paid money for the tickets.

**Option A:** You paid $40 for tickets to see your favorite band

**Option B:** You paid $200 for tickets to see a good band

Most people choose their favorite band in the first scenario, and the expensive tickets in the second scenario. (As you might have guessed, this situation comes from a real lab experiment; it's one of many scenarios that my colleagues tested.)

Nothing has changed about the choice except what you've spent to get the tickets: time in the first case, money in the second. What this and other experiments confirm is what you might expect: we are more sensitive to small losses of money than small losses of time. We feel we've lost more if we choose cheaper tickets than we do if we choose tickets based on working fewer hours. You probably felt this when you were making the ticket choice. *Two hundred dollars is a lot to give up.* On the other hand, *fifteen hours of time isn't that much more than five hours.*

Behaviorally, it's not necessarily rational to make choices this way. We do it anyway, mostly because money is easier to measure. Calculating the value of a $10,000 raise is easy; determining the cumulative value of an additional thirty minutes of free time in a day is more difficult. So we default to the metric that we know for certain.

Put simply, we can account for money, but there's no accounting for time. If there were an accounting for time—if we could say what our time is *worth*—it would be easier to make time-affluent decisions. An accounting for time would make it easier to believe that time-focused decisions carry greater value than the money we might miss out on.

In fact, we actually can begin to account for our time. Part of my research has been devoted to helping people think through how to assign a tangible value to time and the happiness it produces.[58] I'm trying to produce hard metrics for a somewhat soft concept: time value. I'm motivated to create this accounting, because I recognize how hard it is to make time-affluent decisions in the face of easy-to-measure money. Also, I work at a business school full of MBAs with accounting, finance, and investment banking backgrounds. The way to get them to understand and care about their time affluence is to put it in a metric that they care about and understand.

# A New Metric: Happiness Dollars

The metric I've created isn't real dollars, but rather the income equivalent of happiness gains, or what I like to refer to as happiness dollars. I define **happiness dollars** as the income equivalent of the amount of happiness produced by a time-related choice. For example, the happiness you'd gain from a $10,000 raise is equivalent to a decision to use your time in a time-affluent way. You will feel as happy by making that choice as you would by gaining a certain amount of income.

As you might imagine, the process of assigning a tangible value to time and happiness isn't straightforward. First, you must find a representative sample of working adults and ask them how much money they make, how happy they are, and how they spend their time. In these surveys, I identify positive uses of time that people are already engaged in, such as spending time in nature, valuing time more than money, hiring a house cleaner, spending less time stuck in traffic, and spending more time savoring experiences like meals (i.e., the activities from chapter 1). I run a series of statistical analyses on respondents' answers to compare how income influences happiness and how time-use decisions influence happiness. Then I compare the differences between these two analyses to assign dollar values to the happiness gains people receive from time-affluent activities.[59]

It's a lot, I know. To put it into concrete terms, if someone makes $50,000 and receives a $10,000 raise, research suggests that their happiness will, on average, increase by about 0.5 points on a 10-point happiness scale.[60] Similarly, starting to pay to outsource our most-disliked tasks increases happiness by about 0.5 points on a 10-point happiness scale. By comparing these two numbers, I can assign a dollar value to the amount of happiness that this decision creates: about USD$10,000 of happiness for someone making $50,000 year.[61]

We must acknowledge that this process isn't exact. I have rounded the numbers to keep things simple, and I base my calculations on averages; some people will benefit much more or less. The boost in happiness that people get from making time-related choices (or from making more money) varies depending on factors like debt levels, monthly expenses, and income. In fact, people who make less money benefit *more* from making time-related choices. This is because people who are materially constrained also tend to be time poor.[62]

For example, for someone who makes an income of $50,000 per year, the value of spending money to shorten their commute or hire a house cleaner could result in the happiness equivalent of making nearly $40,000 more in household income per year—if they spend at least $150 per month outsourcing their disliked tasks. That same choice for someone who makes $125,000 per year is worth closer to $16,000—still significant, but less so.

The science behind time accounting is still evolving, but we can start to apply this approach as a way to make time value feel more real. Going through the exercise of assigning a tangible value to time-related choices and to the happiness that they produce will help you more easily see that giving up money to have more time isn't always the loss it may feel like. Sometimes—more often than you think—funding time results in a happiness gain that is greater than the equivalent cost to your bank account. And in many cases, spending more money than you think you should in order to fund your time is still worth it. Let's look at some of the happiness dollar values I've been able to assign to various time-affluent activities.

## Valuing Time: h$2,200

Based on making $50,000 in household income per year, shifting your mindset from valuing money to valuing time produces the happiness equivalent of making another $2,200 per year; that's $2,200 happiness dollars. (I use **h$** as a marker for happiness dollars.)[63] Even if you don't change any of your actions, it will help if you simply remind yourself that time (not money) is the most important resource in life.

## Savoring: h$3,600

Spending more time savoring meals is only one way to savor. Savoring all kinds of daily experiences is a path to greater happiness. Enjoying good weather. Listening to a concert in the park. Watching kids play in the street.

Savoring is a form of mindfulness, because it requires you to disconnect from productivity and efficiency and focus on the present. Savoring also requires you to let go of creating the "perfect experience" in favor of creating a good one. In research we call the former types of people **maximizers**, and the latter **satisfiers**.[64] Maximizers stress over which restaurant to go to, what to order, and whether the experience is living up to expectations. In contrast, satisfiers pick a place and a meal without worrying whether they're exactly the right choices. Then they experience the meal without thinking about whether it's what they hoped. In my calculations, shifting from maximizer to satisfier behaviors is worth h$3,600.

## Outsourcing: h$18,000

Many people feel that outsourcing chores is a frivolous expense. Why should we pay for something we can do ourselves? One answer to the question is that the happiness benefits offset the financial costs, to a surprising extent.

Outsourcing your most-disliked task (like laundry, cooking, or cleaning) each month is worth h$18,000. That's a big boost. If you make $48,000 per year, for example, you could hire someone to buy and put away your groceries (something you despise) for about $100/week in most American cities, or about $5,200 per year. That's 11 percent of your take-home salary.

This probably feels completely unreasonable. But when you calculate your life satisfaction boost—h$18,000—the investment seems less excessive:

| | |
|---|---|
| Income: | $48,000 |
| Grocery service: | −$5,200 |
| Remaining income: | $42,800 |
| Happiness boost: | +h$18,000 |
| Income + Happiness Income: | h$60,800 |

What's more, this happiness increase doesn't account for the multiplying effect of spending your newly freed-up time in happier ways. If grocery shopping took 2 hours per week, you now have an extra 104 hours—more than four days—to fill with happiness-producing activities like volunteering, exercising, socializing, or engaging in other hobbies.[65]

Of course, the trick of these calculations is that you must outsource tasks that you do not like. If you enjoy cooking but hate the prep, invest in a meal kit delivery service. If you like cleaning, letting a Roomba vacuum your floor isn't a likely path to greater happiness.

You might be thinking you've found a loophole: I will just outsource my most disliked task and spend this free time working and making money while everyone else focuses on free time and happiness. Clever! But not so fast. As it turns out, working more hours than average, even when we like working, comes at a cost to happiness.[66] Spending an additional eight to ten hours per week working, even on activities we enjoy, results in the happiness equivalent of −h$2,900.

## Chasing Deals: −h$3,300

In this chapter I've observed that, purely from a time point of view, driving around looking for the cheapest gas is a poor use of time. How poor? My calculations show that chasing deals, in person or over the internet, usually isn't worth the time it takes.

We all do it. Nine out of ten consumers seek bargains when they are shopping online, even for inexpensive purchases like toothpaste.[67] For each purchase, consumers spend an average of thirty-two minutes re-searching prices before they follow through. We drive out of our way to save a few pennies per gallon on gas, and we comparison-shop between stores for items we might save only a few bucks on. This costs us about $h$3,300 per year.

## Vacation: $h$4,400

Our most egregious misuse of our time is how we treat vacation days. In my research, the average US employee took off nine vacation days per year. If Americans took eight more days off per year (seventeen in total), it would result in a bump of $h$4,400 per year.[68] Most working adults—even in the United States, where paid time off isn't mandatory—have two weeks of paid vacation available. These data suggest that all people have to do to increase their time affluence and happiness is to take the paid days off they are entitled to.

## Socializing: $h$5,800 or More

We are social creatures, and we're only beginning to understand the steep costs of social disconnection, which is on the rise.

Consider the following scenario: you want to work from a coffee shop a few days a week, and there are two equally close coffee shops near your house. At one coffee shop, you will be left alone, and you'll spend $20 per week on coffee and pastries. At the other shop, you'll know the staff and you will chat with friends, but you'll spend $60 per week. Which do you choose for your happiness?

On the surface, the first coffee shop seems to be the better option, because you'll spend less money and probably get more done. This is a classic case of the money being easier to calculate than the time. In fact, people who take friendly breaks get more done than people who sit alone with nothing to keep them company. You'll spend more money at the second coffee shop, but you'll be happier and you'll likely be more productive as a result. And the happiness you will get working at the second coffee shop is worth about $h\$5,800$ per year.

The math works out:

**Quiet coffee shop**

| | |
|---|---|
| Coffee expense | −$1,040/year |
| Happiness bump | + $h\$0$ |
| Net | −$1,040 |

**Friendly coffee shop**

| | |
|---|---|
| Money spent | −$3,120/year |
| Happiness bump | + $h\$5,800$ |
| Net | + $h\$2,680$ |

It's hard to overstate the value of socializing for your happiness dollars. In the most extreme case, shifting from (a) working all the time and never seeing your loved ones to (b) spending time each day with friends and family produces an income increase that is equivalent to making $108,000 more in annual household income.[69] If all you do is work and you make $100,000, shifting to spending all of your time socializing would do the same for your happiness as doubling your salary would.

These are remarkable values. Of course, they're not realistic examples. Most of us—even if we are really busy—spend at least some time with friends and family, and few of us spend all our time working. But the calculation should give you an idea of how much value your free time can have.

## Active Leisure: $h\$1,800$

Active leisure also pays off. Spending thirty minutes more each day on active leisure, such as exercising or volunteering, is worth about $h\$1,800$

per year. (Even passive leisure, like watching TV or doing nothing, will give you a modest bump of about h$1,000.)

Living with a partner in a healthy and happy relationship is worth h$20,700, which is another reason to prioritize social relationships. Gifts, such as housecleaning, that allow couples to spend more time together create far greater increases in happiness than material gifts; my calculation puts the happiness increase of buying time for our partners at h$4,000 per year.

## Accounting for Time Balance Sheet

It's worth reiterating that the happiness bump will vary depending on how much you earn and your financial needs. Across the board, time-affluent activities produce happiness increases that are often equivalent to thousands of dollars per year in increased income.

Here's a balance sheet encompassing some of the foregoing activities for a person who makes $50,000 per year. These simple strategies result in an expected happiness increase of h$27,500 per year. By employing some of these time-smart strategies, this person will feel the same happiness that would result from a 72 percent salary increase.

| | |
|---|---|
| Income: | $50,000 |
| Shift mindset from money to time | + h$2,200 |
| Take 8 more vacation days | + h$4,000 |
| Savor meals as a satisfier | + h$1,800 |
| 30 minutes per day of active leisure | + h$3,600 |
| Outsource your most disliked task | + h$12,800 |
| Plan how we will spend our free time | +h$3,100 |
| Total | + h$27,500/year |

• • •

The goal of assigning happiness dollars isn't to create precise accounting, but rather to engage in the process of accounting at all. This accounting demonstrates how much more valuable our time is than we might suspect, and how much more money we should spend on time than we do.

Even now, you're likely fighting your brain's effort to convince you this isn't real. You can't hold the value of thirty minutes' worth of socializing in your hand like thirty-six hundred-dollar bills. A certain amount of faith is required to make the leap to time-smart living, but it's worth it. The happiness gains are there, waiting; you only need to get into the habit of netting them.

Let's do that in chapter 3.

## *chapter 2 toolkit*

In chapter 2, I've asked you to reflect on how you typically spend time and identify your most positive and negative experiences. You also learned three strategies that you can use to increase your time affluence: finding time, funding time, and reframing time.

The following exercises encourage you to reflect even more deeply on your daily experiences and to find ways in your own life to find and fund free time.

### Time Tracking

In this activity, you will use the Typical Tuesday worksheet to write down the major activities that you have completed in a typical workday. Then you will plot these activities on the Typical Tuesday matrix. This second worksheet is designed to highlight areas where you could fund or find time by minimizing time spent in stressful and unproductive activities.

### Three Activities to Build Time Affluence

After reflecting on your typical time-use activities, commit to trying three time-affluence strategies, including finding time, funding time, and reframing time.

- **Finding time.** This activity involves removing your most negative and unproductive time-use activities or injecting these activities (like commuting) with happier activities (like listening to music) to make these activities more positive or productive.

- **Funding time.** This activity involves reallocating your discretionary income that you spend on material purchases that don't boost happiness toward time-saving purchases.

- **Reframing time.** This activity involves reframing negative activities like commuting or working in more positive ways—like thinking about your commute as a "break."

# The Typical Tuesday Table

Use the table on the following pages to write down the activities you complete on a typical Tuesday, following the example shown below. It doesn't have to be a Tuesday, but try to make it a workday because this is when you are likely to experience the most stress.

| | Activity | Type of experience | Reason |
|---|---|---|---|
| 1. | The first thing I do after I wake up is put on my favorite music, sit with my partner's cat in our office (Ollie likes looking at the cars below), and drink a cup of dark roast coffee. | Positive experience (pleasurable) | It is something I enjoy. It is relaxing. |
| 2. | Once my coffee has kicked in, I try to write for 1–2 hours uninterrupted. | Positive experience (meaningful) | My brain works best in the morning, so I like to try to get a couple of hours of writing done before meetings. I get cranky when I don't get in a couple of productive hours. |
| 3. | Then I commute to the office. I drive to work around 9:30 or 10:00 in the morning, which means getting stuck in rush hour traffic. | Negative experience (stressful) | It is stressful and irritating, because I feel like I am wasting my time. |

Fill in as many or as few activities as you want, but try to capture the major activities during each period of time shown next. For example, a typical number of activities might be, on average, three to five activities for each time period.

MORNING: WHENEVER YOU WAKE UP TO ABOUT 12 P.M.

| | Activity | Type of experience | Reason |
|---|---|---|---|
| 1. | | | |
| 2. | | | |
| 3. | | | |
| 4. | | | |
| 5. | | | |
| 6. | | | |

AFTERNOON: ABOUT 12 P.M. TO 5 P.M.

| | Activity | Type of experience | Reason |
|---|---|---|---|
| 1. | | | |
| 2. | | | |
| 3. | | | |
| 4. | | | |
| 5. | | | |
| 6. | | | |

EVENING: ABOUT 5 P.M. TO WHENEVER YOU GO TO BED

| | Activity | Type of experience | Reason |
|---|---|---|---|
| 1. | | | |
| 2. | | | |
| 3. | | | |
| 4. | | | |
| 5. | | | |
| 6. | | | |

You can record any additional notes you might have about your activities. For example, you might want to highlight which activities involved time- or money-related decisions (such as the decision to work more overtime hours versus to come home early).

# The Typical Tuesday Matrix

In this exercise, you will try to map the activities that you listed in the previous table onto the grid below. For activities on the positive side of the matrix, use a star or a check mark to indicate activities that you find meaningful or purposeful, not simply pleasurable. In other words, watching TV may be positive, but this activity may also lack purpose or provide little meaning to you. I have given you space to make one matrix each for morning, afternoon, and evening.

MORNING ACTIVITIES

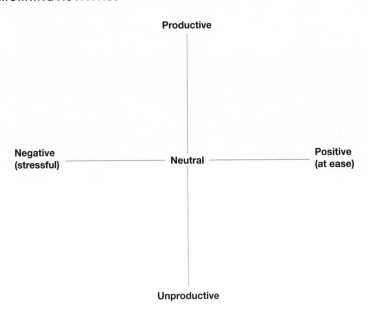

**AFTERNOON ACTIVITIES**

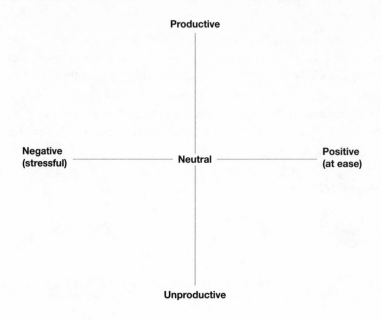

**EVENING ACTIVITIES**

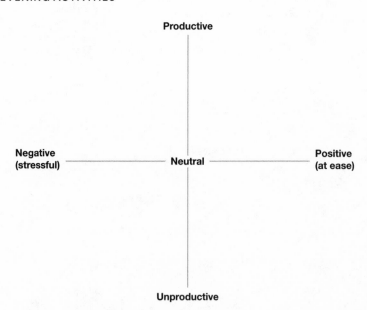

Once you have reflected on which activities are unproductive and stressful, or are pleasurable but not meaningful, you can think about replacing some of these activities with strategies that could improve your time affluence and happiness, as described in the text.

# Find Time: Create a Time-Affluence To-Do List

If you want to use the strategy of finding time, consider adding the following activities to your day, all of which have shown to increase time affluence and happiness.

IF YOU HAVE 5 MINUTES

- Organize the small errands you need to complete, and start checking them off.
- Message someone important to you that you haven't spoken to for a while.
- Check out whether you have any paid vacation days.

IF YOU HAVE 10 MINUTES

- Watch relaxing nature videos on the internet.
- Send a gratitude email to a colleague, family member, or friend.
- Write a journal entry; journaling can increase happiness.

IF YOU HAVE 30 MINUTES

- Go for a walk in nature.
- Do something creative (painting, writing, making jewelry, knitting).
- Read a book (maybe read a book on your phone while in line at airport security).
- Meditate or complete online resilience training (such as through the app Happify).
- Go for a short jog (15–30 minutes).

IF YOU HAVE AN AFTERNOON

- Learn something new (learning can improve happiness).
- Spend time helping other people in your community.
- Plan your next vacation (even planning positive activities can boost happiness).

# The Reframing Time Worksheet

Some activities that you can't find or fund your way out of may seem like time-usurping misery, but there may be value in that time you're not thinking about. By reframing how you think about time, you will feel better about the activity—even if you can't get out of it. List those activities you *must* do that you don't like, try to think of ways in which the time spent on that activity brings some value, and list it in the following table. For example, as mentioned in this chapter, a physically demanding part of your job can be reframed as a daily workout.

| My time-consuming, undesirable activity is . . . | . . . but it does provide some value, such as . . . |
| --- | --- |
| | |
| | |
| | |
| | |
| | |

# 3

# *the time-affluence habit*

Now begins the hard part.

The solutions to time poverty are simple. The execution is something else altogether. Can you make these small daily decisions about time a habit? As with losing weight, knowing what to do is relatively easy. Doing it is harder. And living it every day is the hardest of all.

Even when know we should make time-centric decisions, escaping the allure of money is remarkably difficult. In one survey I conducted, people who said that they valued time more than money still were very unlikely to pay money to outsource disliked tasks, take a more expensive direct flight (versus a cheaper indirect flight), or forgo a promotion to spend more time with their family. In fact, these so-called Taylors made time-centric decisions only about 5 percent of the time.[1]

Let me reiterate: research clearly shows that people who value time are happier, healthier, and more productive than those who value money over time.[2] But we still focus on money, because we underestimate the value of our time; we tell ourselves that we will have more time tomorrow than we do right now (we won't); and we underestimate how long it will take us to complete our daily tasks. We can't help ourselves; we consistently betray the better angels of our nature.

Why? If we have evidence—real data—that tells us the right thing to do, why is it so hard to do the right thing?

Anyone who wants to lose weight will tell you about that struggle. Sugar is bad but alluring. Exercise is good but hard to instigate. We know we should work out, but we could just relax; after all, we're tired and the gym is pretty far away. Parts of our brain drive us to choose vice over virtue. Messages bombard us telling us to do the wrong thing. It's not easy.

And it's the same with time and money. To our minds, money is a need that takes over our attention. In contrast, time is a currency that's hard to grasp and easily ignored.

Our obsession with money is deeply rooted in how we've evolved.[3] Our early ancestors who were successful and thrived learned how to trade. Then they developed currency, a tool that facilitated efficient transactions and allowed humans to proliferate.[4] We are hard wired to think about, worry over, and carefully track finances, because the success of humanity has depended on our ability to access and use goods and money.[5] Some researchers have gone so far as to call money a drug, because its physical effects are similar to those produced by natural and chemical substances in our bloodstream.[6]

People make emotional and seemingly irrational decisions in the pursuit of money. In India, for example, thousands rioted when the largest denominations of the country's currency were replaced with smaller ones.[7] Moreover, friendships—the things humans need most—are torn apart by inequality in financial standing or the perceived poor use of money.[8] After handling money, even six-year-olds will forgo the chance to help. In one study, young children brought fewer red crayons to an experimenter when asked, and they spent more time coloring for pay.[9]

Valuing time seems to stand little chance against the narcotic properties of cash. Yet there are ways we can begin to start seeing time as the more critical currency that it is—and the resource that, more than any other, determines our happiness.

## Prioritizing Time in Our Everyday Lives

This chapter and chapter 4 are designed to help you internalize the good practices I've laid out in previous chapters and build a time-affluence regimen that you can live by. These strategies are designed to help you walk the talk when it comes to treating time as the valuable, precious resource it is.

To make your time-affluent mindset stick, you take three steps:

1. Convince yourself that time is at least as important as money.[10]

2. Remind yourself of your values when faced with critical decisions.[11]

3. Make deliberate and strategic decisions that allow you to have more time across days, weeks, months, and years.[12]

Implementing each of these steps depends on two activities that will become part of your time-affluent life:

1. *Reflection* to create self-awareness about what you're doing and why you're doing it. This seems easy: it's only thinking. But as any behavioral scientist can tell you, we humans are capable of twisting our thinking into Escherian stairwells to avoid uncomfortable or hard-to-accept truths. Your reflection must be intentional and honest.

2. *Documentation* to create a record of your hopes, observations, calculations, and plans for time affluence. Plenty of research confirms the efficacy of writing things down, and it's essential here because of the forces conspiring to make you focus on cash.[13]

Below are specific strategies based on these steps, along with activities for building your time-smart regimen.

# Strategy 1: Address Your Why

How much time do you spend playing Candy Crush or using some other app on your phone? You probably don't know, but it's a habit you've developed in the in-between moments to kill time. For me, it's scrolling through Instagram. Often, I do it when I'm procrastinating on work that's important but not urgent. I see my partner playing games on his phone, too, and I call him on it. He tells me he doesn't realize he's doing it, and, truthfully, I don't realize I'm doing it either. We've both lost many, many hours to idle moments and mindless screen time.

All of us have our own personal Candy Crush behavior, an activity we compulsively, somewhat thoughtlessly engage in. And it's OK. Disconnecting our brains from anxiety and stress can help refresh us, like a sweet snack now and again.[14] But when "now and again" becomes a habit, the activity becomes an unhealthy time suck, disconnecting us from human connection or from better, more time-affluent activities.[15]

## The Small Why Question

One way to beat back bad habits is by asking the **small why** question: *Why am I doing this?*

Be deliberate. It might help to say it out loud to yourself. Follow up with other questions: *What am I hoping to accomplish? Is it truly adding value to my day?* And most crucially, *Could I use this time for something more fulfilling?*

Answer as honestly as you can. Think critically about yourself and your time. And think about the future. Even if an activity is making you happy right this moment, are you borrowing against future time, when you know you'll be more stressed because you're procrastinating now? Think of it like sugar: *It tastes spectacular right now, but if I have chocolate for breakfast every morning, I won't be happy later; I'll have a stomachache, cavities, and five extra pounds.*

If your answers suggest that you truly are disconnecting from anxiety and stress, or that you get genuine pleasure out of the activity, then keep doing it for a bit. Enjoy leveling up on Candy Crush or looking at the latest cute stuff your friends' baby did on the internet. It still may be useful to write down how much time you think would be good to do this before moving on to other tasks. A **small why note** might look like this:

**When:** Tuesday, 9:45 a.m.

**What:** Scrolling through Instagram

**Why:** Stressful meeting at 10 a.m. Need to not think about it for a while.

**Keep doing?** Yes. For no more than 5 minutes. Then prep for meeting.

Often, if you've prompted yourself to think about why you're doing what you're doing, it's because deep down you sense you're not using your time wisely. Maybe you catch yourself watching the next episode of your favorite TV show (a rerun) because it started playing automatically, or you click your way down the rabbit hole of silly YouTube videos, or you find yourself scrolling through a website of pictures of dogs' heads on birds' bodies (it's real).

If your answer to the small why question is, "I'm just filling time" or "No reason, really" or the big red flag answer, "I don't know," stop doing what you're doing. Write down the activity, and add it to a **subtraction list**.

Over time, this list will help you identify the time-impoverishing activities you fall into and may give you insight into why you fall into them. For example, here are a few entries from a friend's subtraction list:

**Subtraction List**

Phone games before meetings

Website surfing before and after lunch

Looking through/choosing Spotify playlists in the morning

My friend recognizes their time-killing activities through the small why question, and a clear pattern is emerging: they mindlessly fill the minutes right around scheduled time. They would do well to add activities that would be a better use of their time, activities they could draw from a **substitution list** like this:

### Substitution List

Phone games before meetings / INSTEAD: Chat with colleague.

Website surfing before and after lunch / INSTEAD: Walk for 15 minutes before lunch; do nothing after.

Looking through/choosing Spotify playlists in the morning / INSTEAD: Get on the road; let Spotify choose playlist.

Knowing why and when you engage in mindless activities can help you replace them with happier time. If you kill time when you're tired, try taking a nap instead. If it's brought on by stress, spend the time planning productive or enjoyable time in your calendar. Is it because you are lonely? Instead of passively scrolling on Facebook—which ironically increases our feelings of loneliness—then text, call, or visit friends or family instead.[16]

Finally, when you're thinking about subtractions and substitutions, it's important to add or subtract experiences in a way that is consistent with your preferences for socializing and working. Unsurprisingly, people who score higher in extraversion are happier spending more time socializing (e.g., eating out); introverts are happier when they spend more time engaging in self-reflective activities (e.g., reading or journaling).[17]

## Strategy 2: Allow (or Schedule) Slack Time

I've discovered that when people begin their effort to find and fund time, they are often so overzealous about replacing bad time with good that they pack their schedules tight with time-affluent activities.

Connie—one of my type A friends—learned a bit about the science of happiness and started to meticulously schedule her leisure time to make sure she wasn't missing out. She would wake up at 6 a.m. on Saturday, try a new recipe, go for a jog while her treats were baking, invite one friend over to try the recipe, and proceed to schedule a packed afternoon of walking, volunteering, reading, and podcasts—often in locations all over the city. Just looking at her social media posts made me feel exhausted.

While I do advocate for spending more time in active and enjoyable ways, my advice doesn't mean you should add so many activities that you spend your Saturday mornings rushing around. In fact, when we stack personal (and professional) appointments back-to-back, we enjoy them less.[18] They begin to feel like obligations, and our stress increases as we try to keep to the schedule. Even putting leisure activities in our calendar can make them less enjoyable.[19] Instead of enjoying a pint with our neighbor, we ignore their story, thinking about whether we'll make the train on time for our next event. We pull ourselves out of the present and into the future, and our worries about what's next start to steal our time.[20]

One way to prevent this is to allow for, or even plan, **slack time**, which is extra time left between appointments that can be used as a buffer or as downtime. Some researchers advocate **rough scheduling**, under which you don't schedule time with friends for 7 p.m., instead planning to meet "after work." Or you'll do gardening "sometime Sunday morning" instead of "from 8 until 10."

Slack time removes the stress of making sure we fulfill all of our plans and allows for spontaneity. This spontaneity matters, because overefficiency carries negative consequences: when we are overly efficient in conversations, we enjoy them less.[21] And prioritizing efficiency makes us more likely to miss opportunities to connect with **weak ties**: people who are likely to bring us creative ideas and new opportunities.[22]

When someone I interviewed named Michael took a few paid days off (to decompress from his overly stressful job), he broke his usual pattern: he didn't try to sneak in work calls or work on reports or be hyperefficient with daily activities like shopping. Instead, he focused on using his time in a leisurely fashion. He was casually grocery shopping on one of these days (he likes shopping) and engaged in the time-affluent activity of chatting up an acquaintance he bumped into there. The chat led to a new job opportunity in a role he felt was perfect for him. The conversation wouldn't have happened if Michael were being hyperefficient and trying to rush through shopping to get to his next work-related task, as usual. Michael attributes this serendipity to being open to using and enjoying slack time.

## Strategy 3: Know Your Calendar Mindset

True rough scheduling isn't for everybody. When conscientious types like me hear, "Let's meet after work," their anxiety levels rise. How can plans be so vague?! Doesn't this mean you may *never* get together with your friends after work? Honestly, yes. And that might be OK. The stress of missing out on roughly scheduled plans is less intense than the stress created by making sure you are perfectly on time for all of your tightly scheduled plans. Even if you can't commit to something as loose as "later in the week," try building in extra time around the activities you're doing. If work ends at 3 p.m. and you're a half hour from where you're meeting friends, schedule the meetup for 4:30 and *don't* schedule anything in between.

If you are still stuck about how much slack time to schedule, you can use your **calendar mindset** to decide how much to schedule.

There are two calendar mindsets:

1. Clock-time people

2. Event-time people

(You can identify your calendar mindset using a questionnaire in the toolkit at the end of this chapter.)

**Clock-time people** use schedules that are defined by the hours of the day—the clock.[23] They don't move on from an activity merely because it feels like the "right" thing to do; rather, they move on because it's 1:30

and that's when they're slated to move on. They are more likely to stick to a routine and set time-dependent goals for their work and leisure (*I will exercise between 5 and 6 every morning*). They make detailed plans for phone calls and dinner dates. (*Our reservation is for 8:15. We will meet at the bar for one drink beforehand at 7:40.*)

In contrast, **event-time people** allow events to shape their schedule. They might set up a meeting, but it will last as long as it lasts; it may run fifteen minutes or ninety, regardless of the scheduled time. Event-timers don't call you at 1:30; they call "when I'm finished with lunch." They're not as concerned about making reservations. They will say, "Let's meet for dinner Saturday night" or "Let's walk home from work when we wrap up for the day."

Most of us can operate in both styles—thankfully, lest workplaces implode.[24] But we all default toward one style or the other, and in our personal planning we need to think carefully about how our default calendar mindset can shape whether and how we account for time and our time affluence.[25]

By scheduling activities in a way that is consistent with your calendar mindset, you will feel more comfortable and will be more likely to follow through on your plans. Maria—a clock-time person—explained how she scheduled her leisure time.

> I love planning and tracking my leisure time to make sure
> I get the greatest happiness from it. After starting fourteen
> years ago (after my first son was born), I still do it. I can't
> imagine not. Tracking my time has enabled my family and I
> to have uninterrupted dinners, road trips, and spend minimal
> time watching TV; we complete arts and crafts in the shed
> (without a TV) instead. Tracking makes sure I don't spend
> time engaged in mindless activities without intention.

Maria makes perfect sense to you if you're a clock-time person. You will be happiest with defined limits, and you will schedule time-affluent activities into your day—including slack time. (Remember, don't *over-schedule*.)

To event-time people, though, Maria's clock-time approach seems almost oxymoronic (schedule leisure?). Troy—an event-time person—explained how he planned his leisure.

> For me, it wasn't about restricting my time in some authoritarian way to be more "responsible" or "less wasteful" with how I spent my time. It was about understanding how I was spending my time in a guilt- and stress-free way. I was able to cut the amount of time I spent scrolling on my phone and watching TV by nearly five hours a week, saving twenty hours a month without having to write it down. My awareness alone allowed me to rein in wasteful [time] spending in a way that felt natural and easy. I could then put this time into things that were important to me—my goals, the goals of my family—and my overall happiness. Those twenty hours quickly added up to giving me the time I needed to start to learn how to ride a motorcycle. I had always wanted to do that but never felt that I had time for it! Being more efficient with my time meant that I was happier overall, saving more time each week, and feeling less stressed about spending time on things that did not bring me joy.

One approach to time affluence isn't better than the other; the better system is the one that matches your mindset. In either case, you need to follow through on your best-laid plans, whether those plans are set by the clock or by the event. Know who you are, and start planning (or roughly sketching out) your approach.

## Strategy 4: Create Intentions

**Intentions** are deliberate actions that force us to think about how we're using our time and to commit to making positive use of it. Subtraction and substitution lists are intentions, in a way. Choosing to read this book is another.

Intentions become powerful when we tie them to daily actions that take our time away. For example, if you want to enjoy more books, you might state your intention as *listen to books on tape.* But an even better one would be to *use my commute to listen to books on tape.* In this way, you've found time and replaced the time-impoverishing activity with an intention for a time-affluent activity. If you want to start writing a book, make the intention to *spend three lunch breaks a week eating and writing by myself.* To increase your chances of following through, put an interesting reminder, such as a bright sticker, on your lunch box.[26] Tying intentions to activities you must complete each day (shopping, commuting, eating) also makes it more likely you'll follow through, because every time you sit down to have lunch, you are reminded of the fact that you could be working on your book.

It will also help to write down your intentions at the beginning of the week and then check them off at the end. If you didn't follow through, write down why you didn't. If you're a clock-timer, you could schedule one hour on Sunday to document and plan the activities you are going to do, and one hour the next Saturday to review whether you followed through. If you're an event-time person, you could plan to use part of Sunday afternoon to think about the high-level goals you want to accomplish with your time for the upcoming week, and also roughly schedule, say, the next Saturday morning, to consider whether you were able to follow through on these goals.[27]

If you're having trouble following through in any of the categories discussed in chapter 2 (finding time, funding time, reframing time), reflect on why you haven't met these goals. Sometimes we don't reach our time-use goals because we are faced with objective constraints: our boss gave us extra work; our dad needed help fixing his computer. At other times, however, we simply don't do what we intended, just as sometimes we don't exercise when we planned to. If you failed to follow through on tracking your time and intentions, a good next step is to employ behavioral strategies to motivate yourself to follow through.

It's time for rewards and punishments.

# Strategy 5: Implement Rewards and Punishments

If your time regimen is going well, plan a reward for yourself. In one extreme case of this, a new initiative—the four-day workweek—rewards employees with Fridays off if they complete their work between Monday and Thursday. Getting to skip work with full pay is, of course, an effective motivational tool. While we don't usually have the ability to give ourselves an entire day off, you could treat yourself to thirty minutes of additional sleep-in time or fancy wine this weekend if you've effectively managed your priorities.[28]

If you're going to reward yourself for following through on your time goals, it's worth remembering a few things about rewards. First, we tend to value rewards earned through effort even when they have no cash value.[29] Badges for hitting certain daily fitness milestones in your fitness app, for example, have proven to be somewhat effective, even though they obviously have no monetary value.

Static rewards—such as always treating yourself with the same restaurant meal each week for hitting fitness goals—will become demotivating over time. It's better to choose uncertain or surprising rewards. One way to do this is to let a friend give you the reward; it could even be a dinner together (thereby adding to your good use of time!). You could also create a lottery-based reward. Suppose you avoid checking email until 5 p.m. three days in a row. Give yourself a 50-50 chance of winning either one fancy coffee or two by flipping a coin. Research suggests that building in a bit of uncertainty about winning smaller versus larger prizes can boost personal commitment.[30]

An even more powerful motivator than earning rewards for good behavior is losing them for bad. Losing has a larger impact on our actions than winning, even when the stakes are low. In one study, people were more likely to cheat when given $30 and told they could lose it than when provided with the chance to win $30.[31] That is, the prospect of losing made cheating more likely than the prospect of winning.

If you are serious about changing your time-use behavior, you may try a strategy that incurs critical costs when you fail.[32] Beyond obvious penalties (no dessert after dinner), technology is here to help you punish yourself more creatively. The application Beeminder takes $5 from your credit card for every goal you don't meet. Another, Forest, provides you with the chance to grow a beautiful animated tree or watch it slowly wither and die, depending on whether you meet your time-use goals. The stickK app lets you set your goals and, if you don't achieve them, allows you to punish yourself by, for example, donating to your least favorite political candidate (a potentially highly effective tactic).[33]

Punishment and reward can take the form of publicity, too. You can share your performance on social media to hold yourself accountable. Public commitment to goals is highly motivating, as is public shaming. Capitalizing on social motivations, such as the need to fit in, can encourage persistent behavior change, which is what we're after—a change that sticks.

# Strategy 6: Engineer Defaults

Engaging in self-control and exerting willpower are hard (and, as it turns out, somewhat overrated). You can get more assertive with your time-affluence regimen by **setting defaults** that produce time affluence. In this way, you don't choose time affluence; it's your default. This means that making a decision means opting *out* of time affluence.

## Make Your Technology Default to Silence

If an app doesn't let you turn off notifications, remove it. Put your device on silent, and commit to checking it only once every three hours, or whatever interval you can muster. (Think of this like physical exercise, too. Start with thirty minutes, then try to go forty-five, then an hour, and so on.)

Be aggressive with this strategy. Unsubscribe from websites that email you regularly. Divert newsletters and other regularly scheduled communications into folders for reading later. You may be surprised how little you miss the notifications. My colleague Davis went as far as to remove all email from his phone. At first, he was nervous about missing important messages, but soon enough he found it relaxing.

> I couldn't believe when I finally would log on and check email how little of it mattered. Not once in the past six months I've been doing this did I feel like I missed something important by not having email on my phone. I figured out if it was really important someone would find me another way. But for the most part, it's so great not feeling that buzz in my pocket all the time.

Davis did a basic calculation. As a college instructor, he received about 200 emails per day during the school year but probably checked his phone when it buzzed, conservatively, 40 times per day. Loosely, he guessed the average disruption was 10 seconds, which totaled nearly 7 minutes per day, or 35 minutes per week, which over a work year equaled about 29 hours. And that's only email. He has since severely limited his notifications from Twitter, Instagram, fantasy football, and news sites (he quit Facebook altogether). He figures he's getting back roughly a workweek a year of his time by defaulting to no notifications and no email.

Fortunately, technologists are recognizing the sapping effect of their wares, and a market has opened for technology that makes it easier to engineer time-affluent defaults. One app, appropriately called Freedom, automatically blocks users from visiting distracting apps and websites, such as social media platforms and online video games. Another, Ransomly, alters the default setting of a room, such as the dining room, to be phone and screen free by using a sensor and app to automatically turn off all devices when they are in the vicinity of the room. In the battle against technology and time confetti, our greatest weapon may be technology.

## Control Your Personal Defaults

You can create a set of rules regarding those activities you automatically won't opt in to when they come up. Default to no for unplanned activities, especially ones for which you're being asked to give up your time for someone else's benefit (or for an unclear benefit), such as a side project at work. Set a quota on work travel (say, one trip per quarter), remembering that you may be giving up advancement at work for happier time, as discussed earlier. Likewise, with personal time, default to saying no when you have a certain number of social engagements already planned.

Engineering the **default no** is a powerful weapon in your battle for time affluence, but most of us are terrible at it. It takes practice. One strategy that will help make it easier is to make default no a public declaration. For example, several of my colleagues already do this by engineering an auto response in email to say, "Thank you for your message; as a rule I check email once a day at 8:30 a.m." Workplaces also play an important role in helping employees feel OK with disconnecting by allowing for interventions, such as giving workers a "Do Not Disturb" feature on their Slack channels.

# Strategy 7: Recognize and Fight Mere Urgency

Sometimes when we are procrastinating on harder, more important activities, such as preparing for an interview, we will waste our time with simpler, less important activities, such as answering email.[34]

It happens to all of us. When we have a busy week at work, with important deadlines, we find ourselves with an inbox at zero. When we feel busy or stressed for time, we also feel an increased sense of pressure to get things done right now. Sadly, this is when we also suffer from a decreased ability to think through the importance of the task we have decided to work on. As a result, we default to thinking about whether or not a task is urgent, as opposed to whether or not it is important. This

FIGURE 3-1

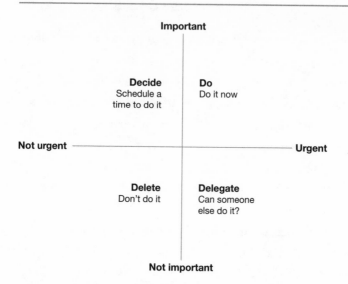

behavior is called the **mere urgency** effect. The matrix in figure 3-1 helpfully summarizes the trap of mere urgency and shows what to do when you face it.

One of the first ways you can begin to stave off the mere urgency effect is to map your activities (something you may already be recording from chapter 2) onto this matrix. Take special care in documenting tasks that, in retrospect, were merely urgent or not important, and try to avoid those tasks in the future when they come up.

You may also recognize patterns. Do you take on merely urgent activities around a deadline, for example, as an avoidance mechanism? Do you succumb to mere urgency when you're tired? Is there one person constantly asking you for favors that are urgent to them but aren't important to you?

## Schedule Proactive Time into Your Life

**Proactive time** (one colleague calls it "pro-time," and we'll use that for its brevity) is time reserved for important but not urgent work (or leisure), found in the upper left of the matrix in figure 3-1.[35]

In general, mere urgency encroaches on pro-time activities the most. Important, urgent matters tend to be taken on with alacrity; unimportant, not urgent things can be ignored (and much of the previous chapters has focused on tactics for doing that).

It's the important activities that we defer when mere urgency surfaces (clean up résumé; write a project proposal; call mother). Clock-time types can set aside an hour for pro-time. Event-timers can plan to do it at some predictable part of the day, such as late afternoon.

Map some of your upcoming priorities on the matrix. For work, these are things you *must* do. For your personal life, it's more likely to be things you *want* to do. Then schedule pro-time into each day for the next couple of weeks, and assign tasks to those time blocks.

Pro-time should be distraction free: this is critical. The merely urgent crops up in communication that interrupts the important things you're doing. So during your daily pro-time, turn off all distractions and block off your calendar so that the merchants of urgency can't spring surprise demands on you. Stay focused on important tasks during this block of time.

Felicia, a senior account executive at a sales firm, does this. She holds a weekly planning session *with herself* every Thursday morning; at this time she moves each of the items on her "important not urgent" list into a block of pro-time she's set aside for the upcoming week. At the end of each week, Felicia fills out a log indicating her success in completing the items on her list.

This worked for Felicia and many other executives like her. In a recent study we conducted with a group of computer engineers, employees who were randomly assigned to schedule pro-time for themselves felt they had greater control over their time and felt they were better at time management. They felt less stressed. They reported being more productive. Importantly for their organizations, they felt happier about their jobs overall. Of those assigned to schedule pro-time, 84 percent said the method should be used across their entire organization.

The key to avoiding mere urgency is to be disciplined about pro-time. Don't miss the scheduled time, and track what you get done. If you lose hours because of an unexpected expense of time, make it up as soon as possible. Follow through—even if you are the only person who will know you did. Think of it as a matter of personal integrity. It's easy to cheat, but don't, or you could end up back where you started in chapter 1, with too much to do and not enough time to do it.

## Strategy 8: Make Leisure Leisurely

It isn't enough to build in more time for leisure. You also must make sure you do everything you can to enjoy the leisure time you have cultivated.

With their kids finally off to college, Miguel and his wife, Alejandra, decided they would take their dream trip. They would tour central and southern Italy for three weeks. It cost a lot of money, a fact they were painfully aware of as they paid up front.

It didn't go perfectly, and, given how much they paid, it was disappointing. Miguel got heatstroke, and they missed a tour of the Vatican. It rained for two straight days along the scenic Amalfi Coast. Alejandra and Miguel fought so much about why they chose this tour in the first place that at one point Miguel threatened to take the next flight home.

Back in America, Miguel and Alejandra looked at their photos— eating squid ink pasta in Venice, walking on beaches along blue oceans, and olive oil tasting in Tuscany. The stress they felt on the trip wasn't there. The missed opportunities somehow seemed smaller in retrospect. They were happy to have gone on the trip. Now their only regret was that they spent too much of the trip worrying about how much it cost versus what they were getting out of it.

You may have had a similar experience. It's not uncommon. Researchers find that thinking about the economic value of our leisure time can undermine our enjoyment of it, because we are constantly comparing the experience against some perceived expected value or ideal.[36] This has been shown in many types of activities: when we track the distance of a morning nature walk, we enjoy the scenery less. When we track the number of calories we're burning during a run, we don't derive as much joy from the experience as we do if we're running to feel good. When we count the number of pages we've read of our latest book, we lose track of the story, worrying whether or not we have hit our reading target.[37] Whenever we "track" our leisure or think about the amount of money our leisure time has cost us, we're like Miguel and Alejandra: we become hyperfocused on time efficiency. Instead of savoring our time, we worry about getting our money's worth from our leisure time.

To enjoy the activities in your schedule, disconnect the value from money and other metrics that don't explicitly measure the value of what you're doing. Turn your thoughts away from, *How efficient was this investment?* to the present moment. Anything that takes us out of our present enjoyment of leisure time destroys its value and makes us less likely to want to engage in the behavior again in the future.[38]

In short, do not think about how much the vacation cost or whether the house cleaner was worth the financial investment. Instead, think about how nice it is to spend extra time with your friends and family— or curled up on the futon enjoying a movie with your significant other.

## Make It Stick

These strategies will provide the foundation for a good time-affluence regimen. You will find more time, and you will enjoy the time more.

I know it's not easy. As someone who continues to struggle to prioritize time over money, I've experienced the battle. I've been caught typing on my computer or taking work calls while (dangerously) crossing the street, eating in restaurants, and at the summit of Mount Kenya (4,500 meters above sea level). I worked for ninety minutes during my best friend's wedding day. I skipped two of my close family members' funerals because I chose to work instead.

Cultivating time affluence requires you to do what I failed to do in those situations: hold yourself accountable. Human nature being what it is, you'll want to take shortcuts, even after reading this chapter and even after coming up with a seemingly airtight time-affluence strategic plan. We are rationalization machines, capable of explaining away bad behavior in a myriad of "creative" ways: *Today was an unusual day, so I don't have to write down the tasks that I completed.* Or *I actually don't mind waiting in line or commuting. It's really not that bad.* One person told me that they would find it "awkward" to have someone clean their house while they were home—even though they hated cleaning, could afford to outsource it, and could schedule the housecleaning service when they were out. Another time-pressed person (a twenty-five-year-old professional) recently told me they could "never" spend money on services that made their life easier, but had "no problem spending a hundred dollars for a new pair of jeans" or $200 a month for a fitness club membership—even if they never used it.

The marginal cost of cheating "only once" seems alluringly low. And these rationalizations are especially likely to intrude in easy moments, when we don't feel great time pressure.[39] On Saturday morning relaxing on the sofa, it's easy to dismiss the notion we won't have time to clean the house later, even though our calendars tell a much different story. The pain of bumper-to-bumper traffic feels less miserable than it is when it's only a topic of discussion during a night out with friends. But the pain will be there for us when we have to clean house or drive to work, and it's massively damaging to our happiness and health.

Even people who are making positive changes in their time use will feel tempted to congratulate themselves too soon and fall back into old habits: *Now that I have gotten the hang of this time and money trade-off thing, I don't need to keep tracking how I spend my time,* or, *Maybe I'll just check a few emails on my phone during my upcoming family vacation; it won't be too disruptive, I'm sure.* As with trying to eat healthy, a few good days makes us feel entitled to treat ourselves.[40] So we get the burger and the milk shake. And the fries. And when we make excuses once, we're more likely to do it again, and we fall back into bad habits.

• • •

Throughout this chapter we've used the metaphors of exercise and healthy eating to describe the kind of commitment it takes to escape your time poverty and live a time-affluent, happier life. The comparison is perfectly apt, but here, at the end, it breaks down a bit.

I'd love to tell you that sticking to a time-affluence regimen creates results you and others can see. Exercise leads to a fitter you, and friends notice a positive change. With your time, it's harder to immediately notice the change. Still, it's there. I've seen it. There's more smiling and laughing, fewer exhausted raccoon eyes, and less fighting with partners and colleagues and kids.

And no matter what you or others see, I promise that if you get into the habit of making time-affluent decisions, you will *feel* it.[41]

## *chapter 3 toolkit*

### Time-Smart Regimen Checklist

Review the eight strategies for getting into the habit of living a time-smart life.

1. **Address your why.** When you catch yourself wasting small moments of free time, ask yourself why you are engaging in this activity. Do you enjoy it, or are you procrastinating on doing something else?

2. **Schedule slack time.** Do not become overzealous after reading this book and try to schedule all the leisure time possible so that not a moment is free. Research suggests that overly scheduling leisure could backfire, because it will feel like work. Make sure to allow for or schedule empty slack time between your leisure activities and meetings.

3. **Know your calendar mindset.** People generally think about time either in terms of clock time (highly specific and set to hours in the day, such as "1 to 2:15 p.m.") or event time (less specific and set to general ranges of time such as "midafternoon"). Knowing your time typology (see the questionnaire later in this toolkit) can help you schedule your time in a way that is most likely to promote affluence and joy.

4. **Create intentions.** To follow through on any new goal, engage in strategies that will help you follow through. Create intentions—figure out who, what, where, when, and how you will increase time affluence—and document your intentions.

5. **Implement rewards and punishments.** Reward yourself when you follow through on your intentions, and punish yourself when you fail. Remember that uncertain rewards are more motivating than static ones and that losses often loom larger than gains, so threatening yourself with a punishment if you don't follow through might help you most.

6. **Engineer time-smart defaults.** Make it easier to engage in time-smart behavior by setting up technology so that it no longer sends

immediate notifications or constantly interrupts. Set "analog" decisions to default to time-smart behavior, too, by, for example, limiting the number of business trips you agree to each year.

7. **Recognize and fight mere urgency.** Recognize the difference between merely urgent tasks and important tasks. Try to focus on the important over the merely urgent.

8. **Make leisure leisurely.** Focus on enjoying leisure moments rather than whether you think you're getting your money's worth from your leisure activities.

# Know Your Calendar Mindset

There are two types of people when it comes to how we think about our time: clock-time types and event-time types. One is not better than the other, but knowing which you are will help you know how to plan your time regimen. To find out if you're a clock type or event type, rate your agreement with each of the following items on a scale ranging from 1 = *Not at all*, to 7 = *Extremely*.

**ITEM**                                                                 **SCORE**

1. When I have more than one task to complete in       _____
   a given time frame, I usually decide to move on
   to the next task only after I am satisfied with the
   completion of the current task.

2. I usually organize my tasks for the day (or week)   _____
   based on the order they should be completed in.

3. I don't mind how long it takes to complete a task   _____
   as long as it is done well.

4. I decide on moving on to my next activity of the    _____
   day only after I am done with the previous one.

5. I decide on moving on to my next activity of the    _____
   day based on what time it is, even if it means
   cutting my current activity short.

6. When I am performing a task with no time limit,     _____
   I check what time it is to pace myself.

7. When I have more than a few items to complete       _____
   in a task, I first determine the amount of time I
   should dedicate to each item.

8. When I make a timetable for a task, I usually stick _____
   to it.

9. When I have more than one task to complete at once, _____
   I usually decide to move on to the next task based
   on what time it is.

10. When I have a task to complete, I decide when to start working on it based on when it is due. _____

11. When I have a task to complete, I decide when to start working on it when I feel I have time to complete it. _____

**Add up clock-time items: 5, 6, 7, 8, 9, 10** _____

**Add up event-time items: 1, 2, 3, 4, 11** _____

Your score on each of the clock-time and event-time dimensions determines what your inclinations are and how strongly they skew that way. If your scores are roughly equal, reflect on *when* you act more like one type than the other, and ask yourself whether there are opportunities for you to more optimally schedule your time at work and outside work.

# The Small Why Worksheet

Use the following template for tracking your activities and having honest conversations with yourself about your time use. Think critically about yourself and your time. And think about the future a little bit. Even if an activity is making you happy right this moment, are you borrowing against future time when you know you'll be more stressed because of what you're doing now? Finally, consider adding the activity to a subtraction list if it's something you decide doesn't bring you value, and write down a substitute, time-affluent activity you can replace it with.

**WHEN: (TIME I NOTICED THE ACTIVITY)**

_____

_____

**WHAT: (ACTIVITY)**

_____

_____

**WHY: (REASON I'M DOING THIS ACTIVITY)**

_____

_____

**KEEP DOING? (YES OR NO; IF YES, FOR HOW LONG)**

_____

_____

**REPLACE WITH? (NEW ACTIVITY)**

_____

_____

# Create Intentions

Intentions are assignments to yourself to fill your days with time-affluent activities. Think of writing down your intentions as creating a time-smart day planner. Set aside time every couple of weeks (clock-time people, set a specific time; event-time people, block off a range of time), and insert activities into your upcoming schedule that will support your effort to improve your time use. At your next check-in with yourself, note whether you were able to do the tasks you wanted to and, if not, why not. Look for patterns that would explain why you did not engage in the behaviors you didn't follow through on, and come up with a game plan for following through on these activities.

PLANNING TIME:

NUMBER OF ACTIVITIES PLANNED:

NUMBER OF ACTIVITIES DONE:

WHICH ONES DID I NOT DO? WHY NOT?

PLAN FOR FOLLOWING THROUGH:

_____

_____

| **Time-affluence activity** | **Time-affluence activity** |
|---|---|
| Activity #1 | Activity #2 |
| When I will complete this: | When I will complete this: |
| How I will complete this: | How I will complete this: |
| Who I will complete this with: | Who I will complete this with: |
| Strategy used: | Strategy used: |

## Time-affluence activity

**Activity #3**

When I will complete this:

How I will complete this:

Who I will complete this with:

Strategy used:

# 4

# *the long view*

Every day you make hundreds of time-use decisions that you can control in the moment. You can put your phone down, stop obsessing about what you'll order for lunch, cancel meetings, and take a walk by a river. You can call a friend, turn off the TV, exercise, and close email in favor of a podcast. These are the moments and actions you've focused on so far in this book.

Some actions, though, are the result of a different kind of decision: a longer life-view decision made years ago that may still carry consequences for the way you spend your time. For example, choosing a job is, in part, choosing a set of activities that could force you into time-impoverishing activities. Decisions about where to live and whom to live with could affect your time affluence for as long as the lease or the mortgage lasts. Having children comes with certain time commitments you must adopt: Should you find time elsewhere, knowing you're going to devote more to childcare?

As important as it is to develop the daily habit of making good time choices, it's equally important to think about the effect on time affluence of major decisions and life planning. You need to look ahead five to ten years and think about how big life choices will influence your time choices.

The goal of this chapter isn't to upend your life or to encourage you to reverse major decisions you've made in the past. If you recently bought a house, for example, you're not likely to sell it right away to increase your time affluence. Rather, the goal here is to explore the nature of the relationship between major life decisions and the ways we plan our time long term. Then, when new life decisions come up, you'll have ways to frame the decisions to be time smart.

## Choosing Jobs

We start conspiring against our own time the moment we enter the workforce. Job decisions, especially early ones, funnel us into a set of behaviors that are destined to make us time poor. They can shape the trajectory and time affluence of our entire lives.[1]

Ted was on the brink of a major life decision that nearly everyone who has worked full time will face at some point: Should he change careers? Ted had worked in retail management for five years since graduating from college. He had a wife and a four-year-old daughter, a mortgage, and many other expenses. It would be difficult for him to take a pay cut. Yet he felt that his job "was like quicksand." As he explained, "The harder I try to get out, the deeper I get in." He felt thankful for having a job but also felt that the constant stress and pressure of driving more sales was driving him into insanity. He was on a promotion track to move up even further at his current job in the next two years. He knew that a career move would involve a pay cut, but he wanted to feel greater happiness and move into a career he thought he would enjoy more, such as being an account executive.

You probably already see the choice here: taking a happier, lower-paying job versus staying at his current job, where his promotion track will sap a ton of hours and result in even more stress.

At different points in our lives we have different priorities, and our time affluence fluctuates. Maybe you've incurred significant loans or have a mortgage and feel the extra money you make in an undesirable job is necessary even if it comes with a time cost—or a cost to your happiness. This is one reason we make time-poor decisions, and there are others. But it's important to know what the consequences are so that you are clear about the effect it could have on your life. We know from research that young people are extremely likely to take the highest-paying job they can. And we know they're not necessarily happier for it.[2]

In recent research, my colleagues and I tracked more than one thousand graduating college students and asked them whether they generally prioritized time or money, using the identical Taylor and Morgan questions I asked you to complete in the introduction. We also asked the students about their life satisfaction and daily happiness. Then two years later, we asked them these happiness questions again.

Two years later, students who prioritized time were happier than those who prioritized money, even when we accounted for how happy students were when they started our study. Why were students who valued time more than money happier? After graduation, these students made their initial career decisions for different reasons. Whether they chose to enter the workforce or enroll in graduate school, students who prioritized time were more likely to report that they were working at something they "wanted to do" as opposed to something they "had to do."

What's more, the time-focused people weren't reporting they were happier because they worked less or made less money: many people who say they value time also report working fifty- to sixty-hour workweeks and are doing well financially. But by choosing time-centric activities and focusing on career decisions that support a time-focused point of view, they set themselves on a long-term path that meant they had meaningful jobs and made time for friends, family, and hobbies.[3]

These findings matter. When choosing jobs, most of us focus too much on salary and prestige—easy-to-measure metrics—and not enough on the value of the time we'll spend in the job or the ways the job will allow us to shape our time outside work. We do this in part because we overestimate the extent to which wealth will make our lives better.[4]

The wealth fallacy extends to work rewards, too. Workers believe that pay, insurance, and other cash benefits like retirement plans will fundamentally determine their job satisfaction. They overestimate money's value.[5]

Simultaneously, they underestimate the value of time-rich features like a flexible schedule or a short commute. Our analysis found that non-cash benefits such as social experiences and paid leave had a greater impact on job satisfaction than additional money. All else being equal, time-centric benefits such as parental leaves, flextime, and sick days contributed to job satisfaction more than receiving an additional $38,000 in annual salary for someone making $48,000 per year. Think about that: a collection of time-smart benefits contributed as much to job satisfaction as a 79 percent increase in pay. These results held even after controlling for income, age, gender, education, industry, firm size, employer type, and firm revenue.[6]

In my research, students who valued time also chose different career paths from their money-focused colleagues. Time-focused students were more likely to attend graduate school. In contrast, money-focused students were more likely to work full time or pursue business degrees. In this study, *why* people pursued their careers mattered more for happiness than what they chose to do. This was true no matter how wealthy students' parents were, eliminating the idea that time-focused people were simply those who could afford to be that way.

One caveat: this study was conducted in Canada, where students graduate with less debt than students in the United States. The results might not be so clear-cut in places where debt loads are higher and loans glower over young workers. That's not an argument against making time-affluent decisions. Instead, it's a signal that organizations and governments could do more to help people feel they can make career decisions for time rather than for money in places beyond Canada, knowing that generally they'll have happier, more productive, and more loyal employees at least two years later. I return to this in chapter 5.

I suspect these findings hold even for decisions that don't involve first jobs. It's in middle career when it is easy for us to become money-obsessed to pay for all that life brings us: mortgages, children, college. We likely have a career established and feel locked in. We may not be able to easily move to the city and take a flexible job for less pay. However, we can at least understand that money-centric decisions don't always work to increase our happiness. And when we're saying to ourselves, *Yeah, it's four hours of commuting a day, but it's $36,000 more a year,* we should realize that our time is probably worth more than the money.

Ted, whom you met earlier, chose to stay at his stressful job. Two years later, he was making more money; he was also divorced, living alone, and unhappy. When the job choice is in front of you—when you are faced with a critical juncture in life—it is important to think about the happiness you might lose throughout your life if you choose having more money over having more time.

## Choosing Where to Live

Commutes suck. And they're getting worse. The average commute time in the United States is twenty-six minutes each way (a 20 percent increase from the 1980s). Certain mega-commuters commute ninety minutes or longer each way to work.[7] I've done the math in chapter 2. Mega-commuters burn weeks of their lives in high-stress, unhappy gridlock. In one research project a person complained, "One of the things that I hate most is my daily commute. I have come to dread this daily ritual. Every morning and every afternoon, I have to steel myself for what feels like going into a battle that I am doomed to lose."[8]

Commutes are the space and time between work and home.[9] Bad commutes are, generally speaking, the by-product of a disconnect between one's desire for a certain type of work and one's desire for a certain type of home. We want good jobs that are largely located in concentrated economic zones, and we want big houses that are at least a car ride away from those jobs.[10]

I've talked about the desire for high-paying jobs and the reasons we tend to overestimate the value of salary and bonuses for our happiness.[11] With housing, our focus on status and materialism can often drive our desire to live in bigger homes farther away from our jobs.[12] Again, we're undervaluing the time we lose connecting between life and work.

Ironically, we frame our desire for certain kinds of housing around the idea of affordability, even if it's costing us massively in the time (and happiness) we lose by paying less for a place that demands a longer commute. When deciding where to live, most people focus on the features of the house, as opposed to the features of life the house will dictate.[13]

Often, you get more for your money when you live farther away, but even that hackneyed phrase betrays a financial-centric point of view. In truth, whatever value you get for your money, you may lose in time.

It helps when you're faced with these decisions to reframe them as trade-offs between features of your home and your time. Take this example. You can move to a suburb and get a 2,700-square-foot, five-bedroom home with a large backyard and a garage for $400,000. The commute is seventy-five minutes one way. Or you can move to a 1,400-square-foot, three-bedroom condominium with a driveway but no garage, and no backyard but a park within walking distance from your house, also for $400,000. The commute is ten minutes by car or bike.

By moving to the city, you pay the same money but lose two bedrooms, a backyard, and a garage. Yet you gain twenty-two days (more than five hundred hours) to use in ways other than commuting. Suppose you plan to live there for at least five years. When making your purchase decision, then, the calculation isn't how many bedrooms you're paying for at one place versus the other, but rather whether the extra two bedrooms, a backyard, and a garage are worth the 110 days of your life you'll lose to commuting over the next five years. Would you give up, or *pay*, three months out of sixty—5 percent of your time—for two bedrooms, a backyard, and a garage?

Although many people look forward to waiting until their "golden years" to ditch their commutes, this example and my research suggest we need to think seriously about ditching our commutes now and find housing closer to work, or work closer to housing. If you can't move right now, work from home at least occasionally if you can. For workers with moderate commutes—a total of one hour per day—working from home one day a week instantly buys you back two days of the year.

I recognize that the choice of where to live involves more than square feet and lawns. School districts, family, a partner's job, and general preferences for the environment we want around us all play important roles in this major life decision. My aim isn't to suggest that the decision to buy less house closer to work, or to take a lower-paying job closer to our house, is an easy one, or even necessarily always the right one.

What I want to do is empower you to overcome your inclination to think of this challenge primarily in terms of money-for-features. Instead, think about your choices from a time-centric point of view. If you can't make an obviously beneficial switch in housing in the short term, you can use the strategies discussed in chapter 2 to make the commute more bearable. You can listen to your favorite podcast, meditate, or plan for your upcoming day—or maybe even shell out the cash to spend one or two days commuting to work via a ride-share service.

And then, when the next chapter in your life arrives, you'll think differently about the decision of where to live or work and possibly make a different choice that could foster happiness and time affluence.

## Planning Your Time

This book is full of time-positive strategies for you to employ. You may have already begun feverishly injecting time-affluent activities into your life: nature walk every Thursday at 4 p.m. Call stepdad every Saturday morning at 11. Ride share to work every Friday and listen to podcasts. If you're a type A you may already have a packed schedule of activities that promote time affluence (while always remembering to leave slack time, as I talk about in chapter 2).

Bravo! Keep at it! But (you knew there was a *but*) planning time-affluent activities over weeks, months, and years will require additional tactics. For the effects of time-affluent activities to hold, you must think about the need for variety and spontaneity.[14]

We tend to underestimate how quickly the joy of any new activity will dissipate.[15] Back to the diet analogy. It's harder to stick with it if we're bound to a protein shake at 6 a.m. and spinach salad at 1 p.m. Every. Day.

## Variety Helps

When we spend time throughout our days and weeks doing many different things as opposed to many similar things, we feel more productive, less stressed, and happier. In contrast, doing things repeatedly or for too much time—even positive things like socializing—can create stress and unhappiness. Some data show that people who spend more than three hours per day in the company of others report higher stress and lower happiness than people who spend less time in the company of others.[16]

In another study, researchers sent text messages to people throughout the day and asked them what they were doing and how happy they were. People who responded to more than 60 percent of these text messages saying that they were in the company of other people reported higher stress and lower happiness—no matter how much they said they derived joy from the company of others. Even the extroverted among us need a break from others.[17]

This makes sense. Too much of a good thing dampens its effect.[18] To recognize their value, you need time away from carefully planned, time-positive activities. If every moment is about maximizing time happiness, none of them are about meaning, or even about earning a living.

It's good to plan time-affluent activities into your life; try to vary the activities and avoid their becoming routine. As noted in chapter 3, allowing for spontaneity helps, too. If we adhere too closely to our plans, we could miss the opportunity to create our own luck. Richard Wiseman, a psychology professor at the University of Hertfordshire, finds that one of the key distinguishing factors between lucky and unlucky people is that lucky people are willing to deviate from their routines and keep an open mind.[19]

In one of Wiseman's experiments, participants were asked to flip through a newspaper containing photographs and count the number of photographs. Three pages in, there was an ad that read, "Stop counting, there are 43 photographs in this newspaper." A few pages later, there was another large advertisement that read, "Stop counting. Tell the experimenter that you've seen this ad and win $235." Lucky people—people who didn't just simply do as they were told and continue mindlessly counting the photographs—were more likely to win the money because they approached the task in a more flexible and open-minded way.[20] In Wiseman's words, "Lucky people just try stuff. Unlucky people don't do anything until they walk through every single angle and by then the world has moved on." As this study emphasizes, leaving time in your life to go off script is likely to pay dividends.

## Saying No

If we too rigidly plan our schedule and lock in predictable uses of our time, we risk missing the serendipity that's necessary to transform our careers and lives. Spontaneous conversations, unexpected meetups, and whimsical decisions to take an afternoon off carry value. But we can't do it all the time. We can't say yes to every networking opportunity and conversation. If we did, our days would be overrun with distractions, and we would be stuck in the trap of prioritizing only what's right in front of us (the urgent and unimportant) at the expense of focusing on what truly matters (the nonurgent and important). We need to develop long-term policies for how we approach demands on our time, with an emphasis on how to productively say no.

Monica's unique solution to this dilemma is to always say yes to a conversation, while being more cautious about saying yes to an action. Monica runs her own boutique marketing agency that employs about twenty graphic designers and copywriters. She often feels that she must be working all the time to bring in new business and manage her team. Constantly strapped for time, she has read many self-help books about time management. Most of these books advocate developing a single strategy: learn to say no.

At first, Monica thought that saying no made sense. She'd think, *When people email me inquiring about my services, I'll simply say no to a conversation if I have already met my sales quota. If they want to talk about owning a small business, I have a set answer I give them about why I can't do that.* However, she always felt a bit uneasy about turning away people who were genuinely interested in connecting.

Monica changed her tack after taking an improvisation class; improv is notable for forcing participants to say yes to all ideas they're presented with and working with them.[21] To invite moments of spontaneity and serendipity into her life, she decided to say yes to an initial conversation with people who inquired. At the same time, as a rule, she would plan to say no to anything beyond a conversation. What's more, she stacked all the resulting "informational meetings" on one day in the middle of the week. This would break up her nine-to-five weekly grind and ensure that these meetings didn't distract her from doing important but nonurgent work like completing client projects.

Over time, Monica's business and social network expanded and flourished. Although she was careful not to take on work that would overstretch her team, saying yes to conversations allowed her to have more time for spontaneous connections. One of these conversations led to a partnership with another design firm. Another conversation led to the hiring of a new, up-and-coming design star. Still another caller became a client of the partner of one of her employees, who specialized in ad copy for biotech companies.

Monica explained:

> By saying yes to every conversation or idea, just like I was taught in improv class, I have been able to let a lot more success into my life. The best part? This success doesn't just benefit me. It also benefits the people I work with. Through these conversations, I have been able to help my employees find new jobs for their partners or themselves, I have noticed

opportunities in the market to take on new and different work, and I have found new staff to take on different kinds of work that I only ever dreamed of completing. . . . So my rule today is that I say yes to the idea or conversation, and more often than not I say no to the implementation (unless the project or profit margin is too good to turn down). But when something interesting comes my way that I can't take on, I think about whether someone at my firm or one of my friends could benefit. Then I forward the opportunity to them. This way, I don't feel overwhelmed, and the people who work with me are provided with a worthwhile opportunity to test their skills.

Monica's time strategy is grounded in behavioral science. Delegating and forwarding tasks to others not only help us deal with our workload and feel greater control over our time but also make the people around us feel appreciated.[22] Moreover, helping other people feels good.[23] By providing instrumental opportunities for a junior colleague, we have engaged in an act of prosocial behavior. When we help others, we help ourselves.

It's not hard to see, though, that this approach might get out of control. Saying yes expands your network, meaning you'll get more requests to talk, and at some point you're going to have to say no, even to a conversation. You need strategies to do that well, too.

## Don't Use Time Excuses

It might seem natural to refuse a request by telling other people you're too busy. Unfortunately, time-related excuses have a high social cost. My colleagues and I have found that people who make time-related excuses are perceived as less likeable and less trustworthy than those who do not.[24] This is because time is perceived as under our personal control: all of us, even the busiest person in the world, get the same allotment of twenty-four hours in a day. It comes across as a personal preference not to use your time on your colleague's request.

Instead, people respond much more positively to those who decline requests using excuses related to money or energy, or provide no excuse at all. So if you really must say no to a conversation, a meeting, or a request from your boss or a colleague, try to make it clear that the reason is something outside your personal control, such as family obligations or unexpected travel.

## Ask for More Time

Instead of saying no, you can ask for more time in order to make taking on a request more viable. At work, deadlines are a major source of time stress. A simple, powerful tool to feel more in control of your schedule is to push back adjustable deadlines. This sounds easy, but we often avoid requesting extensions because we worry it will make us appear less competent and unmotivated.

My data shows we overestimate the likelihood we'll be perceived in this way.[25] As long as we request more time to work on tasks *before* the deadline has passed, most managers actually believe we're more motivated when they get the request. It's likely that your colleague or manager will grant you an extension unbegrudgingly. In contrast, when we feel stressed but fail to ask for more breathing room on flexible tasks, we end up submitting suboptimal work. We feel dissatisfied, and we end up disappointing our colleagues and our managers—the very thing we were trying to avoid.

Another form of the extension request is to ask for a few days off to reduce stress and make sure you're operating at a high level when you're working. Burnout produces bad work and demoralized workers.[26] A few days of paid vacation is preferable (and less costly) to an employer than your failing or quitting in frustration.[27]

One person who's faced this tension is Wanda, who confided in me that she felt overwhelmed as an assistant in an oncology doctor's office. She was paid to work four days a week but often worked five days to keep up with the demands of the growing practice. She didn't take time off and often worked through weekends and holidays. Her adult daughter, Leah, asked why Wanda wouldn't ask for a raise for the extra hours she was working, or at least for a few extra days off. "I don't want to hassle my boss," Wanda told her daughter. "I know how busy she is." In truth, Wanda worried that her boss would see this as a sign that she couldn't do the job; Wanda feared she would be fired at a time when she felt she had few other employment options.

Several months later, Leah found Wanda exhausted and in tears at her living room table, trying to fit in a few more hours of work before the two went out to enjoy a Saturday morning together.

Wanda had had enough. But she wasn't going to ask for a raise or for days off. She was going to quit. Leah walked in as Wanda was writing a resignation letter. Leah wanted to take a different approach. She suggested they write a less intense email instead.

In this email, Leah helped Wanda factually report that she was working eight to ten additional hours each week that she wasn't getting paid for. She reported that she felt it would be fair either to be compensated for these hours or to have five days of paid vacation over the holiday to rest and recover after having worked so many extra hours.

Her boss quickly replied. She had no idea Wanda had been working so many additional hours. The boss told Wanda to bill her for any extra hours she worked each week going forward. Wanda also received five days of paid vacation immediately (and a gift certificate for a spa!). The boss told Wanda that she would find another assistant to cover her hours while Wanda enjoyed her vacation. They also set up a meeting to discuss the possibility of hiring another part-time assistant to help one day a week.

Wanda's fear of saying no turned out to be misplaced. Her fear that her boss would be disappointed was wrong. Most people I have interviewed about time affluence forget that we can also negotiate for time at work, just as we can negotiate for a higher salary.

Shamefully, employers often don't tell workers whether their deadlines are flexible or whether they can ask for more paid vacation. As a result, the most time poor among us—junior employees and women—are the least likely to ask for more time. But they should. For

years, negotiation scholars have been researching the best way employees can ask for more money; workers can and should negotiate for time
just as aggressively.[28] You may be surprised how receptive managers
are. In truth, the costs of losing an employee are far higher than granting a short vacation or a modest raise. Wanda's boss didn't want her
to leave any more than Wanda wanted to quit. What Wanda's boss did
want was for her administrative tasks to be handled competently, and
for Wanda to be a happy employee in a job she loved.

Of course, some workplaces are unwilling to accommodate time flexibility or consider such requests seriously. If you're searching for a job,
make it a point to ask about these policies, and look skeptically at companies that don't consider these issues or seem to be confused by your
question (suggesting they haven't thought much about the value of your
time). Still, the number of firms across sectors that are willing to work
with you on this is growing; it must, as the battle for talent becomes more
intense. Helping workers live time-rich lives can be a recruitment tool.

## Evaluate the Opportunity Cost

To help you say no, remind yourself of the opportunity cost of saying
yes. Saying yes to a meal with someone who wants to network with you
is saying yes to sixty minutes in addition to the time you'll spend getting to and from the restaurant and finding parking. If you budget
two hours total, you should ask yourself, *What am I not doing with that
time that I could be doing?* And what is the effect on the time around
that meal? Did you have to rush to complete tasks? Did it increase your
stress trying to make the appointment, and did it affect your work
afterward?

Similarly, work travel is never only the days you spend away from
home. The day before your trip you have to do laundry (thirty minutes), iron (thirty minutes), pack (twenty minutes), and negotiate your
trip away with your partner and family (sixty minutes). That's 2.3 hours
devoted to your trip before it starts.[29] On the day of the trip, you lose
an hour or more traveling to the airport, and from the airport to your

travel destination (forty minutes). Once you arrive there, you will have more meetings than you expected and likely have a late-night flight back—which could be delayed, resulting in your feeling exhausted the next day.[30] And the day after, it takes more time to unpack and reorient yourself.

When looking at your schedule and planning your activities for the next several months, be sure to add these kinds of incidental time costs surrounding the activities you said yes to. Write down a list of five to ten things you won't be able to do because of these time costs. If you travel a lot for work, you probably won't be able to be a mentally available parent to your kids on the day you come home from work. You will miss family breakfasts, phone conversations, and recitals. You will also miss lazy evenings together with your spouse or quiz nights at the pub with your best friend.

Quick lunches, dinners, and trips seem trivial, but over the long term they can come at a major cost to your social relationships and your health in a way that's worth accounting for. Some dinners are necessary, and some work trips required. But saying no, even a few more times a year, is likely to bring positive change.

## The Big Why

In chapter 3, when developing strategies for living every day in a more time-positive way, I told you to ask yourself the small why question. At any given moment, *Why am I doing this?* Now I want you to address the **big why** question, which focuses on what you value as a person over a long time. The big why question is, *Why does prioritizing time over money matter to me?*

The answer to this question will motivate you to keep pursuing better uses of your time. It may not be a simple answer, and it may change over time, but it's important to periodically reflect on it.

As I reveal in chapter 1, I'm bad at prioritizing time more than money, in part because I grew up in a working-class family where a focus on increasing the money we had was palpable and where I was taught that leisure was lazy. As I have grown older, I've tried to reset my thinking about the true value of my time—in part by accounting for time, holding myself accountable for having more and better time, and by answering the big why question.

For me, the answer to this question involves my cousins Marc and Paul.

My family is small and scattered. I don't have siblings. Most of my cousins were married with kids when I was young, except for Marc and Paul. They were a few years older than me, and we managed to get into plenty of trouble together. Marc and Paul taught me to swear. (I remember particularly the education I received from Blink-182's hit album *Take Off Your Pants and Jacket* and reruns of *South Park*.) They also taught me about online dating and professional wrestling. When we weren't raising hell, we talked about their favorite soccer teams, and we talked about my upcoming soccer tournaments.

We talked about my tournaments because Marc and Paul couldn't play soccer. At age six, they were diagnosed with Duchenne muscular dystrophy, a horrible and rare degenerative genetic disease. Only a handful of families in North America had more than one child with DMD when Marc and Paul were born. By the time I was watching *South Park* by myself, they were using wheelchairs. When I graduated from college, they couldn't breathe on their own. When I received my PhD, they were quadriplegic. Two years later, they died in short succession. Marc and Paul remind me that our time is finite—and we don't really know how finite. I do not want to let time pass unremarkably or, worse, wastefully.

In *Stumbling on Happiness*, Harvard professor Dan Gilbert quotes Willa Cather:

> One cannot divine nor forecast the conditions that will make happiness. One only stumbles upon them by chance, in a lucky hour, at the world's end somewhere, and holds fast to the days as to fortune or to fame.

If something makes us happy or gives us purpose, we need to hold on to it. We need to do whatever we can to prioritize it, to care for it, and to not let distractions disconnect us from it. All of us are living lives that are slowly slipping away. In an era of constant distraction, without careful planning our seconds will pass easily, and unhappily.

So whenever I find myself mindlessly checking out during a work task or scrolling on my phone for what seems like hours, I remind myself of the big why, my cousins, and the slowly fading nature of life.

In fact, to make these reminders easy for myself, I have my cousins' initials tattooed on my wrist. I'm not saying you need to take it this far; a photo in your office or a note on your desk will do just fine. Having Marc's and Paul's initials on my wrist gives me the motivation to keep going, to keep prioritizing my time, and to take ownership and responsibility over the life I want to live.

The ultimate motivator is knowing the answer to your big why and following through on implementing positive time choices. Take a few minutes to reflect on your big why. When you've done this, put a reminder someplace where you often find yourself squandering time, such as the office or the living room. Whenever you need a reminder of what's important, it should be easy to spot.

● ● ●

Becoming a time-affluent person over the long term takes practice. You will do better during some periods, and worse in others. Some stretches may feel overwhelmingly positive, and others may feel like a slog to maintain your focus on time.

That's expected and OK. Keep at it. You got this.

Best news of all, you'll likely get better at it as you get older. We've seen via research that older people tend to be Taylors more than Morgans. They tend to be more financially secure, making it easier to value time.[31] Then there's this: older people have less time left. (Other research suggests time seems to move faster the older you get, so we feel the loss of time more acutely.)[32] Time is literally scarcer and more valuable as we age, so making the decision to value time over money becomes an easier calculation.[33]

No matter your age now, with this chapter and the preceding one, you have tools to become happier through better use of your time, both in everyday moments and over longer periods.

In chapter 5, it's time to give your bosses some tools to help you, too.

## *chapter 4 toolkit*

These tools will help you navigate upcoming major life decisions and learn to think about the potential effect on your time over the course of years when you're making big decisions.

### Five Time-Affluence Habits

Following are strategies that are proven to help you lead a time-affluent life over longer periods of time.

- **Vary your activities.** The effect of time-smart choices will lessen over time if you do the same thing every time you have an opportunity. When planning time-affluent activities, spend time throughout your days and weeks doing many different things.

- **Say no.** Set default responses to certain kinds of requests that you get often and that cause time stress. Practice saying no to requests you don't think you will have time for. Try saying yes to requests for conversations, but no to requests for actions.

- **Ask for more time.** Many requests don't have hard deadlines. If you think that having more time would improve the quality of your work, ask for it. If you need a vacation or are feeling overwhelmed, tell your boss.

- **Remind yourself of opportunity costs.** Whenever we say yes to something (travel, additional work projects), we say no to other things—spending time with family, going to kids' soccer games, helping our parents. Before saying yes, calculate not only the time costs but also the opportunity costs to help you decide whether the decision you are contemplating (e.g., additional work travel) is really worth it.

- **Ask yourself the big why.** When making major life decisions, you should ask yourself what you value. What is your purpose, and why does prioritizing time matter to you? Put a physical reminder of your big why somewhere where you can see it. In this way, you will be prompted to think whether any decision you are making in the moment aligns with your overall goals and purpose in life—whether it aligns with what truly matters.

# Major Life Milestones Worksheet

In the leftmost column of the table below, list the major events in your life, especially ones involving money, such as choosing a job, choosing where to live, getting married, moving in with someone, having a child, buying a puppy, or taking care of a family member. Account for some of the time implications of your expected decision by documenting those costs in the middle column. For a job, this might be the length of the commute and the amount of travel required. For getting married, it might be the amount of planning required.

After you have thought about the time costs, consider how you might offset some of these costs—either by making a different decision or by increasing your focus on time-smart strategies such as funding time, finding time, and reframing time. Write those strategies in the last column.

| Major life decision | Estimated time costs (day/week/year) | Strategies to offset any time costs |
|---|---|---|
|  |  |  |
|  |  |  |
|  |  |  |
|  |  |  |
|  |  |  |

# Saying No Worksheet

Plan to say no by creating a policy for committing to requests for your time. It could be like Monica's, where she said yes to requests to talk but no to requests for action.

**WRITE YOUR GENERAL POLICY HERE:**

_____

_____

_____

_____

_____

Now write down some standard answers you can use when people ask for your time but you can't or won't give it. Keep in mind that time-based excuses like "I'm too busy" or "I don't have the time" are not good reasons, because they tend to make others think you are less likeable and less trustworthy.

**REASON NUMBER 1 TO SAY NO:**

_____

_____

**REASON NUMBER 2 TO SAY NO:**

_____

_____

**REASON NUMBER 3 TO SAY NO:**

_____

_____

# Asking for More Time Worksheet

In addition to planning to say no, you should plan to ask for more time when you need it. You could be like Wanda, who asked her boss for more time in the form of paid days off. Write your general strategy for deciding when you will ask for more time (at work and outside it) and how you will ask for it.

_____

_____

_____

_____

Next, write down some standard reasons for asking for more time when you need to complete tasks. Keep in mind that people are more favorable toward granting time when you ask well in advance of a deadline, or when you ask for more time for a justifiable reason. As with saying no, reasons such as "Because I don't have the time" are not likely to provide good justifications.

**REASON NUMBER 1 TO ASK FOR MORE TIME:**

_____

_____

**REASON NUMBER 2 TO ASK FOR MORE TIME:**

_____

_____

**REASON NUMBER 3 TO ASK FOR MORE TIME:**

_____

_____

# Big Why Worksheet

Use this space to create the answer to the big why question: *Why does prioritizing time over money matter to me?*

_____

_____

_____

_____

_____

Your big why can be an event in your life that reminds you of how precious time is, or a long-term goal you have that requires you to not squander your time, or something else. Use your answer as motivation in moments when you know your time is being used poorly, or to remind yourself of the importance of valuing time over money. Finally, revisit your big why question periodically and update the answer if you need to.

Now use the space that follows to generate ideas for how you will remind yourself of your big why in daily life. I got a tattoo to remind myself, but, of course, how you do this can be as simple as putting up a photo in your office that reminds you of what truly matters.

_____

_____

_____

_____

_____

# 5

## *systemic change*

*Time is the most precious commodity—let's see if we can
find ways to give our fellow citizens more of it.*

**—CASS SUNSTEIN, PROFESSOR, HARVARD LAW SCHOOL**

This book is for you, so to this point I've focused on you: what you do
with your time, what you can change, and how you can change it.

But it's not entirely your fault that you feel time poor. Social structures
promote time poverty. Our organizations and their human resource
policies, and our public institutions and their structures, contribute
substantially to this modern affliction.[1] As much as you can change, so
can they. This final chapter is for them.

More specifically, it's meant to enlist you in a broader effort to engage
leaders in creating time-friendly policies for workers and citizens. This
chapter will feel different from the others; it is built to make a case for
change rather than to help you institute personal change. I felt it was

important to include this chapter, because we can't fix the time-famine epidemic without the help of leaders and government. It is my sincere hope that you will dog-ear this chapter and hand it to an HR manager or local government leader.

• • •

Companies and the government inadvertently and intentionally perpetuate time poverty. Each year, US companies waste $100 billion in employees' time, and the government imposes 9.78 billion hours of paperwork on its citizens.[2] In the United States, for example, "free" programs—like FAFSA (Free Application for Federal Student Aid), Medicaid, and SNAP (Supplemental Nutrition Assistance Program)—impose a "time tax" on eligible recipients, requiring them to complete complex and lengthy paperwork.[3]

Around the world, international aid programs require recipients to walk for miles as a way of "proving" they need the help.[4] In one study, nonprofits asked potential recipients of food aid to walk more than four miles to receive aid, instead of the one mile they were typically asked to walk. When the distance was increased, fewer people sought the food aid even though they needed it, and richer people weren't less likely to come.[5]

In an increasingly noisy, crowded, and busy world, institutions can help us value time and become more time affluent. Organizations can help employees see time off as something to celebrate; governments can help citizens save time by offering subsidies to live closer to work; new technologies can help people disconnect from their online news feeds, coordinate their commutes, and more cheaply and easily outsource tasks to others. Nothing is stopping our institutions from increasing time affluence for workers and citizens. Leaders need only to decide to make it happen.

# Work Policies

## Wasted Time Increases Stress and Resentment

The digital transformation of work is probably the single biggest factor in creating our modern time famine. At the highest level, it has created new norms of occupational instability. To offset the effect of these changes, many employees have improved their skills at great cost, accruing debt. This debt, combined with the fear of losing a job in a volatile market, conspires to make us focus ever more on earning money at the expense of time. The tools that enable the digital workplace have also shredded the time we have into smaller pieces of confetti, each of which has the potential to pull us back into work and away from time-enriching activities. Work has never loomed larger in our minds.

Work also excels at wasting our time. Harvard Business School professor Teresa Amabile and University of Texas at Austin professor Andrew Brodsky studied more than one thousand employees in twenty-nine occupations, including lawyers, managers, and soldiers. More than 78 percent of the employees they studied said their organizations "systematically wasted their time" by keeping them idle between meetings and assignments. Converting this wasted time into wages amounted to more than $100 billion lost in unproductive wasted time each year.[6]

Workplaces also create time poverty by imposing unnecessary administration. Doctors spend 8.7 hours per week (about eighteen days per year) billing and record keeping; this number has doubled in the past decade.[7] Business professionals spend an average of twenty-three hours a week (forty-eight days per year!) trapped in meetings—up from ten hours a week in the 1960s.[8] CEOs, who presumably have complete control over their schedules, report "wasting" 57 percent of their workdays engaged in activities that have "absolutely no impact" on the missions of their companies.[9] And it isn't only high-earning professionals who feel this way. In a survey of more than seven hundred average income earners (who made about $50,000 per year), 99.9 percent said they were routinely asked to complete unimportant tasks that wasted their time, such as unnecessary phone calls, emails, and paperwork.[10]

Wasted time causes stress, too. One employee, Corey, confided his latest work-related conspiracy theory: he thinks his boss holds meetings each week for the sole purpose of creating work that doesn't need to be done. At one of these meetings, his colleague Heather became so frustrated she dug her nails into her palm until she bled. Drawing blood was seen as a better alternative than screaming about the ridiculousness of her latest assignment: creating a fifty-page report about a discontinued workplace policy that (most likely) no one would read.

When forced to wade through workplace drudgery, we're reminded of other tasks we could be doing, increasing our time stress. We feel the opportunity costs viscerally.[11] Whatever annoying task we are doing is preventing us from the main point of our job (e.g., seeing patients, helping customers, fixing problems). We think, *Why bother doing soul-crushing tasks when I could be doing something better with my time?*

The advice to leaders here is obvious: don't assign time-wasting activities. Better yet, recognize those time wasters and institute time-affluent replacements. Reassign a weekly meeting no one finds valuable as mandatory "walk outside" time. Encourage idle time to be used as social time. As Chandler Myers, a former military veteran, recounted to me, "Something as simple as grabbing lunch with a colleague can be immensely important. When my colleague started to encourage this, my morale and the morale of my team brightened. All of our tasks became more manageable, because we knew we always had these small social breaks to look forward to."

## Financial Incentives Exacerbate Money-Centric Thinking

HR policies play a significant role in shaping how employees perceive their time. Financial incentives are a cornerstone strategy for improving performance, and they work—to an extent. But we now know that financial incentives carry costs that may outweigh the productivity gains.

In a large-scale data set that my colleagues and I analyzed, we found that performance incentives may have the power to change how employees use their time.[12] Employees who were paid for their performance spent 2 percent less of their time each day socializing with friends and family. In contrast, they spent 3 percent more time socializing with customers and coworkers. This difference was true no matter how many hours they worked or what industry they worked in. While these differences seem small, they add up quickly. It's equivalent to spending thirty minutes less per day on personal social connections that generate happiness, and forty-five minutes more with colleagues, clients, and other connections that don't increase our happiness. Quick math: that's 120 hours (five days) less time with friends and family per year, and eight days more with clients and colleagues.

The effect is especially pernicious for nonsalaried employees.[13] Hourly workers are more likely to think about time as equivalent to money and are more concerned with wasting time, saving time, and using time in "profitable" ways.[14] As one lawyer explained to me, "Billing hours creates an adversarial relationship with time. I often feel like if I do something other than work for an hour, I have to pay that hour back later. So, to not feel like I am in 'time debt,' I often forgo leisure altogether."

John, a personal trainer, explained to me how this time-as-money thinking was a major demotivator—even in a career he loved. "I used to work for a company that told me to think of every person who walked through the door like a number. My boss said, 'John, it is simple. The more clients that come in and the more they come in, the more money we make.'" But John hated thinking about people (who were coming to him for help with achieving their fitness goals) as dollar signs. "This people-as-cash mentality made me anxious. I didn't want to seem pushy. As a result, I stopped talking to clients. I was worried that they would see me as a money-hungry trainer, instead of someone who truly cared about their success."

John quit after six months and went to work at a smaller gym without commission. Ironically, his sales went up 300 percent. "Now that

I am not focused on thinking about how to squeeze as much money as I can from every person who walks through the door, I can spend more of my attention on doing what I do best—empowering people through strength training." Encouraging employees to focus on cultivating social relationships will certainly reduce the employees' stress, but it also could improve the bottom line.

A simple shift away from focusing on billing and compensation would be a massive boon to organizations' plans for their human resource departments. Society already does a great job of making us overly focus on money. Employees don't need another reason to think about their time as money. Taking employees' time off the clock is a good first step in helping cultivate time affluence.

There are many other strategies HR leaders can take.

## Reward Employees with Paid Time Off

Workplaces can help employees find time by rewarding them with it. In the United States, one out of four private-sector employees receives no paid vacation.[15] Yet we know that employees who are offered (and take) all of their paid and unpaid vacations are more engaged, creative, and productive than those who do not.[16] They derive more meaning and satisfaction from their jobs.[17] After taking a vacation, most employees report feeling less tired and more energetic, and they more readily savor daily experiences.[18] Even short vacations can have benefits lasting up to two weeks.[19]

One long vacation is less beneficial than many shorter ones, so HR departments should help employees take getaways and award them with short stints away from the office.[20] In a survey of 148,000 employees, only those who regularly took vacations experienced any benefit of doing so.[21] This is because after two weeks, our after-vacation blissed-out feeling evaporates and we go back to being overscheduled, over-committed, and burned out.[22]

In addition to offering time off, companies should mandate workers use it, by any means necessary. Unused vacation is a particularly

American scourge: in one survey, 75 percent of employees did not take all of their paid vacation days.[23] More than 700 million vacation days go unused each year—5.6 billion hours that could be spent on time-affluent activities instead of work.[24] That's a lot of untapped happiness. It slows the economy, too. Researchers estimate that unused vacation takes $255 billion of spending out of the economy each year. To put this statistic into perspective, consultants estimate that the cost of all cars bought in the United States in 2019 totals $462 billion.[25]

What's more, when workers do take vacations, they feel obligated to spend some of that time working. Most American employees feel compelled to work during vacations (Hello, from Portland, Maine!).[26] Working on vacation increases stress and creates time confetti, forcing employees to jump between worlds and mindsets.

Employers: tell your workers who don't take their vacation, "If your boss left you a giant stack of money sitting on your desk one morning, you wouldn't walk away from it. But by failing to take all of your paid vacation, that's what you're doing—walking away from a gift of time worth thousands of dollars."

Or you could force vacations upon your workforce. In an extreme example, Shashank Nigam, CEO of SimpliFlying, an airline marketing consultancy, forced his employees to take one week off work—paid—every seven weeks. He also forced his staff to disconnect from work. If an employee checked their office email, Slack, or any other work-related communication platform, Nigam *took away their pay*. The company was serious when it said the time off was mandatory. What did it find?

After their vacations, employees' creativity increased by 33 percent, their happiness increased by 25 percent, and their productivity increased by 13 percent. Since that small experiment, SimpliFlying has made some modifications to the original plan. These mandatory vacations now happen only every *eight* weeks, and employees who work on the same projects can't take their week off consecutively. Beyond these minor modifications, the company is still following through with this policy.[27] As it turns out, companies don't suffer when employees are well rested. They thrive.

Vacation offsets mental health issues as well. In a representative survey of 3,380 working adults, taking ten additional paid vacation days predicted a 29 percent average drop in reported depression overall, and a 38 percent drop in depression for women with children.[28]

## Offer Time Rewards

Smaller time rewards in lieu of minor performance recognition cash awards can also help HR departments combat time poverty. Funding free time for workers through services like TaskRabbit and Uber rather than the occasional $200 cash card is a positive change that could increase workers' time affluence.

That is, if they use them! As with vacations, workers also fail to redeem time-saving vouchers. Data from 207 companies (with 200,000 employees) shows fewer than 80 offered time-saving options for redemption. Of those that did, only 3.2 percent of employees redeemed their points for time-saving rewards, whereas 67 percent of employees redeemed their reward points for material items, such as books.[29] I suspect this is because employees often view these rewards as luxuries, especially when compared with the material purchases they could make with cash or credit gift cards.

One potential solution to this aversion is to limit employees' reward choices to decisions that are focused on *positive* time. Researchers at Stanford conducted a pilot study in which doctors were rewarded with vouchers for time-saving services. The program gave credit to physicians who were completing tasks not always formally recognized, such as supporting a colleague, volunteering to teach in someone else's course, or mentoring a student.[30]

As one doctor explained, "If I volunteer to teach in someone else's course, I get credits and can use those credits to order groceries because I don't have time to go to the store. You can also use the credits to get grant-writing support or help with presentations when you're giving a lecture. These vouchers really help to restore my time." One physician used these credits to help his pregnant wife after she gave birth.

Another donated some of these credits to a colleague who would be "picking up the slack" while she was out of the office.[31] Doctors who involuntarily received these credits reported higher work–life balance and less intention to quit.

Another way to get employees to redeem time-saving vouchers is to assign time-based rewards a cash value.[32] To help employees take paid vacation or time-saving rewards, organizations can appeal to employees' money-first mindsets and make time savings *seem* financial. As one Silicon Valley HR leader suggested to me, "To better motivate people to apply for jobs that tend to have lower pay and more vacation time, we should show the total compensation package, not just the salary, putting a value on health care, child care, public transportation subsidies, vacation, and sick leave, and calculating it all. That way, employees will know what they are truly paid."

To test whether putting a dollar figure on noncash rewards increases employees' interest, my colleagues and I conducted eight studies with more than three thousand Americans. Prospective employees were asked to choose between nearly identical jobs:

$100,000, with two weeks of vacation

$90,000, with three weeks of vacation

Three-quarters chose the higher-paying job. But there's another way to look at this by looking at the salary value of the vacation:

$100,000, with two weeks of vacation (valued at $3,846 in salary)

$90,000 with three weeks of vacation (valued at $5,192 in salary)

In the second scenario, the number of employees who chose the higher-paying job dropped to 50 percent. A similar effect was found when benefits other than paid vacation (e.g., health care) were shown as line items and given a value. (Note: this doesn't seem to work with lower-paying jobs at entry level, where workers are far more money sensitive.)

Marketing time as money therefore seems to be a crucial talent re-cruitment strategy: job seekers reported that they thought those em-ployers truly cared about employees and were more considerate of work–life balance. And companies could enjoy an additional upside: increased diversity. Women often see high-powered jobs as equally at-tainable but less desirable.[33] This simple and costless intervention could draw more women into the applicant pool by making a company seem more family friendly and licensing employees to take all of their paid vacations or take any time-saving rewards that are offered.

This book isn't meant to deliberately highlight gender issues, in part because I find that men as well as women benefit from valuing time over money. However, these findings suggest that women might be par-ticularly likely to benefit from time-related HR practices, especially to the extent that women still take on the majority of the childcare.

## Let Workers Ask for More Time

As much as workers feel compelled to not use their vacations, they're similarly reticent to request more time *at* work, fearing that it will make them look incompetent and unmotivated. In ten studies with employees and managers, my colleagues and I found that employees who felt time poor avoided requesting deadline extensions—even when these dead-lines were adjustable. They would rather hand in suboptimal work than ask for a few more days to work on required tasks.[34]

Of course, avoiding extension requests can undermine employees' performance. In one experiment, we assigned business school students to write a paper and gave them a flexible due date; if students needed more time, they could email the instructor to request an extension without penalty. Students who had requested an extension turned in higher-quality essays and received higher grades from a professor who was not aware of who had received assignment extensions.

Women and junior employees are especially unlikely to ask for more time, because they worry about the way such a request will be perceived. This tendency is tied to data that show women and younger workers tend to be more insecure about their positions at work and more socially focused.

The key to combating this reluctance is to normalize the behavior. Broadly, it's important to communicate the fact that asking for more time—to try to balance the demands of work and life—is OK. Employees who are overwhelmed and who are secretly desperate for more time on a project need to be told they aren't alone. Deadline extension requests (and requests for vacation time) often occur in private, such as over email or during one-on-one conversations. As a result, employees are likely to underestimate how common these requests are. They also underestimate how much other employees experience similar stressors.

Employers need to let their workers know they're not alone and that taking extra time is normal. Communicating the prevalence of granting extensions could be an easy and powerful way to reduce employees' fears of being singled out as incompetent and unmotivated.

Often the strictness of a deadline is ambiguous: employees may not know whether the deadline is movable. When facing this ambiguity, most workers will avoid asking for more time in case the deadline is inflexible. (Again, it's worse for women and younger workers.) When assigning tasks, managers should clearly communicate whether or not a deadline is adjustable.

## Let Workers Work Anywhere

Companies that let workers decide where and when to do their jobs—whether in another city or in the middle of the night—have workers who are happier, more productive, and less likely to quit.[35] Research by my colleague Prithwiraj Choudhury found that employees with work-from-anywhere arrangements were 4.4 percent more productive than employees with a more traditional work-from-home policy allowing them to work whenever they wanted to but requiring them to live closer to the office. The research team estimates that this productivity gain could result in an average $1.3 billion boost to the US economy each year.[36]

The policy produces other indirect benefits as well: employees benefited from bringing their salaries to places with lower costs of living, such as Florida. They also spent less time commuting. Each employee in the study (there were six hundred in total) drove an average of eighty-four miles less, reducing emissions by 44,000 tons during the study. It's likely that employees also felt less stressed and happier given the increased control they had over their time.

Of course, these employees worked in specific jobs for which such an arrangement was possible. And this strategy wasn't without its drawbacks. Some employees didn't like the feeling of being left on their own and missed the social connection element of their workplaces. Researchers suggest that periods of in-office work, or "sprints," could help all employees build a strong foundation of trust with their supervisors and each other. Conversely, sabbaticals—a long-standing academic perk—are proving increasingly popular in companies. Early research shows they benefit both the worker and the company.

For HR and workplace leaders, a mindset shift is in order that may feel uncomfortable but is backed by data: you will gain better talent and more-loyal employees by helping workers increase their time affluence. It is easy for managers to lose sight of the fact that the best data shows that employees who take the most time off (and ask for extensions when needed) are the happiest and most productive.

• • •

A final note on work policies that encourage time affluence: leadership is crucial. Managers must lead time-off trends by practicing them. By saying, "I would like to take more time and put more thought in my response to your proposal than what we had originally discussed," managers can help employees feel more comfortable in asking for extensions themselves. Managers also set the tone when it comes to bad habits like working while on vacation or not taking one. When you send work-related emails when you are supposed to be on vacation, you send a strong signal to your subordinates that they should always be available, too. Don't do it.

If you email an employee late at night, early in the morning, or on a weekend, be clear about why you are emailing at strange hours and whether or not you require a response. I learned this the hard way when I (inadvertently) sent a panic through my research team by emailing at 3 a.m. when I was traveling. One student immediately texted another, wondering whether I required an immediate response. They lost sleep over an email that was not urgent. I should have led by example. I could have added a short note at the beginning: "I'm traveling, please ignore this email until normal work hours" or, better yet, not sent it at all. The entire point of email is that it's asynchronous and doesn't—shouldn't—demand immediate attention.

## Public Policies

We know from data that those who benefit the most from making time-saving purchases are those who make the least amount of money. Time poverty is worse for the financially impoverished.[37] They spend more time commuting, working multiple jobs, and waiting for services than the wealthy. It's a tricky paradox, because we also know that those who make less money are less likely to invest in free time and are more likely to think they can't afford to buy time. My studies suggest we should spend more money than we think to buy back time, even when our means are limited.

Unfortunately, our social structures exacerbate this paradox, creating time poverty for those who need the most help getting rid of it. The United States, for example, is the only country in the industrialized world without paid maternity time off, leaving most new mothers scrambling to figure out how to find time *and* money for childcare through a combination of disability, vacation days, and paid help. The United States also has the least-generous benefits for, and the lowest public commitment to, caregiving.[38]

Let's look at some ways governments could ease the burden of time poverty for their citizens.

## Reduce Paperwork

To receive permits, licenses, tax deductions, subsidies, educational assistance, and health benefits, citizens must fill out forms, travel to government offices, and wait. In Washington, a policy that was recently implemented meant that families who wanted Medicaid would need to complete up to thirty-one pages of paperwork. Officials learned that busy poor families couldn't keep up with this complex paperwork. The result: a huge drop-off in the number of applications from eligible families that needed the coverage. For lower-income Americans faced with unpredictable work schedules, unreliable transportation, difficulty in finding childcare, and a lot of stress, it can be impossible to overcome bureaucratic hurdles.[39]

As Harvard Law School professor Cass Sunstein argues, "Excessive paperwork requirements do not merely take time. They impede infrastructure improvements. They increase poverty. They reduce economic growth. They make it difficult or even impossible to get access to opportunities and benefits that could fundamentally change people's lives."[40]

## Create Time-Saving Aid

To examine the benefits of reducing time poverty among the working poor, I have been conducting a large-scale study in one of the largest and poorest slums in the world, Kibera, in Nairobi, Kenya. The women who live in this slum spend forty hours every week on chores and other forms of unpaid labor. Hand-washing laundry and watching it dry (so that it doesn't get stolen) takes up to ten hours a week. Even in this slum, where women earn an average of $5 a day, there is a market for time-saving services, along with lessons for all public policy officials about the value of people's time and the ways officials can support time affluence for all citizens.[41]

In Kibera, women sometimes fund their time, paying nearly half a day's wages to others to do their laundry or take clothes to a local laundromat. They also pay others to purchase vegetables for them to save the hours it would take to walk to and from the market. As Gladys—a single working mom living in Kenya on less than USD$5 per day—explained to me, "Hiring someone to go to the market for me saves me time that I can use to rest, spend more time with my kids, or spend more time selling vegetables at my stand. To me, it is worth the cost."

Even though these services are clearly desirable (even for these women who are struggling financially), time-saving services for the poor are often undervalued by potential aid recipients themselves and by the policy makers building supportive programs.

I asked a group of forty aspiring policy makers at the Harvard Kennedy School's program in public policy which of two aid initiatives would be more likely to improve women's welfare: one that would save working women time, or one that would provide them with cash. Only 10 percent said that the time-saving initiative would be more effective. When I explicitly provided students with the choice between three policy programs (a program that gave cash, a program that provided prepared meals, or a program that saved time), only four respondents (13 percent) selected the time-saving program; 87 percent chose cash.

Luckily, nonprofit organizations are starting to recognize the importance of time-saving services for women working in poor countries worldwide. In 2016, Melinda Gates wrote a "Gates Note" on the issue and created a video "Time Poverty: The Gap That No One Is Talking About," highlighting the fact that in every part of the world women spend more time on unpaid work than men. She observed that the "massive hours that girls spend [on household tasks] distorts their entire lives." Building on this call to action, nonprofits are starting to provide time-saving services to women in hopes of increasing their time affluence and downstream educational attainment.[42]

OneProsper—a nonprofit organization I work with in India—provides rainwater collection technology that eliminates six to eight hours per day of travel to collect water. This nonprofit also provides girls with bikes so that they can get to school faster. This assistance increases the number of girls and women who can attend school. As one thirteen-year-old, Bhomi, said to me, in response to receiving the bike and water technology, "Not having to collect water has reduced water-fetching drudgery. I am now studying in ninth grade. It was almost impossible for me to go to school on foot. The bike has changed my life and I am able to continue my studies. Thanks to these donors, I can read, go to school, and my entire life has been transformed."

## Make Vacations Mandatory

Historically, the policies of most governments have focused on improving material prosperity.[43] Indicators like the gross domestic product (GDP, the monetary value of the goods and services produced in a country) have been considered the main indicator of societal well-being, because of a general belief among policy makers that wealth results in greater happiness. More recently, governments have started to recognize that other factors can shape citizens' well-being, such as how optimistic they feel about their lives, the amount of air pollution they experience, and income inequality in society.[44]

One factor to date that policy makers have overlooked is time affluence, or the lack of it. Using a database of seventy-nine countries, a collaborator and I analyzed the relationship between time affluence and happiness. Countries with a higher proportion of citizens who valued leisure more than work were happier, regardless of the type of government in place or the relative wealth of the country.[45]

People who lived in countries that were more time focused (versus money focused) were happier, because they were less impacted by financial concerns. After the 2008 financial crisis, the GDP of the United States fell 4.3 percent—as of this writing, the largest decline in the post-world war era. Following the meltdown, major depressive disorders and stress increased, while optimism and happiness decreased.[46] People in the United States, and worldwide, who found meaning outside work and were more time focused than money focused showed less of a negative shift in happiness or stress.[47]

Policy makers need to ask whether there are ways for them to shift citizens' time and money orientations to improve time affluence and promote happiness. Can we measure well-being in ways beyond GDP and then act to increase those measures, just as we act to increase productivity and retail spending (which, in fact, may be tamping down our time affluence and happiness)?

The percentage of people who value leisure more than work varies wildly, from 40 percent in the Netherlands to 1.2 percent in Tanzania. More generally, in areas with chronically high levels of income inequality and in poorer areas—such as Latin America and Africa—fewer citizens value leisure more than work.[48]

These results suggest that the existence of policies that encourage citizens to make time-related decisions can make for happier citizens. In organizations, incentivizing employees to take their paid vacations, implementing aggressive family leave policies, and even shortening the workday could be vital for improving health and happiness. The Gothenburg City Council in Sweden, a top 10 country in the *World Happiness Report*, recently switched from an eight-hour to a six-hour working day. Employees who took part in this experiment were happier, less stressed-out, and more productive, and they took less sick leave.[49]

## Update Urban Planning

The ultimate time suck is the commute. One entrepreneur, Aslyne Rodriguez, started EmpowerBus to provide workers in underserved communities with better access to public transportation.[50]

The service—funded in part by employers and employment agencies—finds time for low-income workers by providing reliable, on-time transportation for their (often lengthy) commutes and allowing them to reassign that time in time-affluent ways, whether that is to take classes (upgrading high school or taking college classes), develop a skill, or relax and listen to music. Suddenly, an activity that was encouraging time poverty is being used to enrich lives. The venture is now extending its ability to find and fund time by delivering groceries to workers on the bus. Now the time that people spend shopping is freed up, too, a benefit that is significant for many lower-income people who live in food deserts and have few viable options for healthy eating that don't take a lot of time out of their day.

As one woman living in Ohio explained, "I don't have a car and try not to walk to the store because my neighborhood lacks sidewalks. I have to access a grocery store with a pharmacy because one of my children has special needs. Prior to EmpowerBus, I would cab myself to the grocery store fifteen times or more monthly. It was very expensive as the cab rides were as much as $8 each way." EmpowerBus not only gets her from point A to point B but also helps her unload her groceries. She saves a lot of money, too: thirty taxi trips at $16 used to cost her $480 per month, or $5,760 per year—nearly one-third of what she paid for rent for the year. In contrast, the bus is free, and, although it takes slightly longer, the time cost is neutralized through the grocery delivery service.

Governments can also do what they do best: regulate through penalties and incentives to encourage, or sometimes mandate, different behaviors. Apps can help solve some issues by rerouting people to less-congested areas or even helping them decide when to travel. This is good! In 2018, Americans lost an average of ninety-seven hours a year due to traffic congestion, costing them nearly $87 billion (or an average of $1,348 per driver).[51] More recently, apps are matching people for carpooling. This service saves time and improves the commute: making social connections and talking to people we don't know well increases happiness, reduces our stress, and expands our social networks.

But the vast majority of people don't use ride-share apps (only 36 percent have *ever* used them) and instead drive alone to work (76 percent).[52] With one of my students, I recently conducted eight field experiments to try to encourage employees to carpool to work using one of these technology-based platforms. All eight experiments failed miserably. Of eighty thousand employees, we only successfully encouraged twenty-two new users to try a carpooling app.[53]

Through regulatory policies—such as congestion pricing and parking bans—governments could prod people to use these services. The cost of implementation could be well worth the benefit of removing millions of hours of commute time, taking cars off the road, and increasing people's positive use of their time.

## Recognize Time's Value

Governments can also enlist design teams to rethink bureaucracy that usurps valuable time. Services that let us order our coffee ahead of time and pick it up can be applied to public services as well. For example, in 2016, Philadelphia's Penn Medicine Hospital hired a diverse team of physicians, health economists, and designers to solve major bottlenecks in service delivery.

The team members focused on "stripping processes down to core functions" to "clarify the complicated."[54] In the words of one of the participating staff members, "In our modern world, it is easy to junk things up. Simple is hard. We are quick to add more questions to research surveys, more buttons to a digital interface, more burdens to more people. Yet more words, screens, pages, boards, or tasks are seldom the answer." They usually take up more time. Rethinking service delivery can likewise free up hundreds of thousands of citizens' hours.

• • •

Choices about time, whether voluntary or constrained, define the health, well-being, and economic opportunity of everyone in society. Any time that we spend stuck in traffic is time that we can't spend enjoying our families, contributing to our communities, working, or developing ourselves. A lack of free time—or even a perceived lack of time—predicts poor health. As you have seen, these feelings affect all of us, from parents with young children living at home, to those who are working multiple jobs to make ends meet. Time poverty even affects students, who are increasingly crippled with debt and face heightened competition to succeed at work, therefore combining intense study schedules with full-time work.

Workplaces, organizations, and governments need to be part of the effort to make us all time smart. To start, they need more data. A good amount of data on individuals and their time use is amassing, but little data exists at the organizational, municipal, or country level. (I am working on this now; let me get back to you in, say, five years or so.) Better measures of time use in large-scale panel data from all over the world—not just wealthy countries—will drive conversations about time poverty in local and national governments. And we need more organizations to take time poverty seriously as a public health issue that affects not only individuals but also the well-being of a company, a city, or a country. Without a concerted effort, time poverty will remain a barrier to happiness and economic mobility for nations around the world.

Still, there's much to be done right now, and I've highlighted many of these ideas here. One more thing we can do is to lobby our companies and our public officials to recognize the problem. Now that you recognize your own time poverty and are trying to take small, simple steps to change it, we need to push our institutions to do the same. When it comes to finding creative solutions, individual action is not enough. We need a paradigmatic shift. In the words of author Anne Helen Petersen, "Reducing societal-level stress and burn-out requires institutional change. It isn't something that an oxygen facial or a treadmill desk will fix."[55]

Amen.

# time in the future

*How did it get so late so soon?*
*It's night before it's afternoon.*
*December is here before it's June.*
*My goodness how the time has flewn.*
*How did it get so late so soon?*

**—DR. SEUSS**

The future of time is filled with promise and peril.

You've come a long way in understanding some fundamental truths about time, money, and the modern world. Time poverty matters, materially. We know this. We have the data. We know that the so-called Easterlin Paradox is true: the accumulation of wealth does not always create an increase in happiness. Chasing professional success at all costs is a cause of, and not a solution to, our feeling of having too much to do and not enough time to do it. And there are attendant consequences of living this way: depression, obesity, loneliness, selfishness—the list goes on.

We have started to acknowledge these truths, and we're toying with interventions, at both the individual level and the policy level, to overcome time poverty. Some places are trying four-day workweeks (the United States, as with paid parental leave, lags behind).

It's a good start, but we need to go much farther, lest the 80 percent of Americans feeling time poor rises to 90 and then to 100. We need to test interventions beyond the typical white-collar ones to help workers at all economic levels and in all types of jobs, including the professions where it is seemingly difficult to make time-smart changes (for, say, teachers or health care and service workers).

We need to convince business leaders that time affluence is a competitive issue. The war for talent will demand that companies take time affluence seriously. The assumption that there's a return on treating workers well hasn't always been a given. It has been built and is continuing to be built over time, through experience and data. We need to extend these discussions by proving the return on time-affluent work policies. This work has already begun.

We need to scale interventions to help whole societies shift their focus away from success equaling economic growth and toward other measures, including the way they value time for individuals. We need to acknowledge the real and significant costs associated with the cultural obsession with financial growth: rising health care costs, an inability to retire that creates a lack of growth avenues at work, and a dearth of social participation.

Policy changes could facilitate the changing of social norms. If the United States made paid vacations mandatory, the economy would benefit, fundamentally shifting the rhetoric around what matters. I call this legitimizing leisure. We know that countries that value leisure more than work are happier and are better able to handle the emotional consequences of financial shocks like economic downturns. We know that happiness increases productivity. So the natural by-products of turning the cultural norm inside-out—from a money-driven society to a time-smart one—would be higher productivity and lower health care spending. Shifting the rhetoric could be contagious in a way that social scientists are discovering is quite powerful. We look to others to see how we should act.[1] Policies that help some enjoy their leisure fully and positively will make other people and organizations eager to emulate.

Also, innovators must push technology in directions that will create time-affluent outcomes at all levels of society. Autonomous products, such as self-driving cars, can also promise time wealth for the already relatively well-off, as long as these devices coordinate commutes and do not increase congestion. Broadly, automation promises ever more remarkable time savings and can be engineered in ways to help the neediest and most time impoverished among us. I think of the poor women I've worked with in India and Africa: a basic washing machine—that stalwart robot many people take for granted—provides these women with thousands of hours of time to devote to education and childcare. And it creates security and empowerment that improves their station and the overall well-being of their region.

This is a future we should all be able to get behind. I will use my data, and will collect more data, to help create a time-affluent future for all. In the next ten years, I see reducing time poverty (in addition to material poverty) as a crucial component of tackling our most wicked problems, including educational inequality, obesity, and climate change. I'm serious about this, and I hope you are, too.

Because it starts with *you*. That's why I wrote this book primarily for you, the individual. It starts with becoming time smart, recognizing the profound effect that this transformation has on you, and then demanding that others respect and accommodate your approach to your time.

• • •

As I write this, my colleagues and I are mourning the passing of Clayton Christensen, the legendary, masterful Harvard Business School strategy professor. His theory of disruptive innovation, it's not hyperbole to say, was one of the most important business ideas of the last half of the twentieth century.

Sitting down to finish this concluding chapter, I revisited Christensen's classic *Harvard Business Review* article "How Will You Measure Your Life?" (July–August 2010). Its themes and ideas are consonant with what you've just read here: think about the purpose of your life; make a strategy for it; be deliberate; don't expect money and professional success to make you happy.

When he wrote the article in 2010, Christensen had just beaten back the cancer that would return and take him from us a decade later. His confrontation with the inexorable truth about time—it's finite; you never get it back—helped him see, feel, and *live* by the tenets in his article.

> I have a pretty clear idea of how my ideas have generated
> enormous revenue for companies that have used my research;
> I know I've had substantial impact. But as I've confronted
> this disease, it's been interesting to see how unimportant that
> impact is to me now.

I have offered a lot of scientifically rigorous strategies in this book. I am a time nerd, after all. And I know you are incredibly busy. I hope that the time you've invested in reading this book has convinced you that time poverty matters to you. I hope it has created the space you need to think about the purpose of your life and to put this purpose into action.

I hope, too, that it's clear to you that seeking time affluence isn't selfish. In fact, it's entirely the opposite. When you have put thought into who you are and why you do what you do, and when you have shaped your time so that you can act in a way that is in line with your values, the entire world profits.

We may be destined to become, at some point and to some degree, the plaintive narrator of Dr. Seuss's impeccable lyric at the beginning of this chapter. But there's so much more we can do now to create a happier world and to live, individually and collectively, time-smart and fulfilling lives.

We simply have to decide to do it, before the time has flewn.

# *frequently asked questions*

My colleagues, students, dinner guests, and family members, as well as the occasional Uber driver, consistently ask me interesting questions about time, money, and happiness. This appendix addresses a few of these questions that come up most often. Because these responses are meant to be brief, I have provided additional resources for more information.

## Is Time Versus Money Really an Individual-Level Decision?

Whether we are rich or poor, married with kids or single, younger or older, we see that valuing time over money is linked to greater happiness. Yet people ask me an important question: Doesn't our social context matter for our decisions and happiness? Readers often inquire about whether and how their partners, workplaces, and kids shape their time–money choices and happiness. And they are right. Our social context shapes every aspect of our time and money decisions (and every other decision in life).

When we become parents, our children (and even our pets) shape the amount of time available to us each day, as well as our decisions about money versus time. Retirement alters the amount of free time available to us and the ways we use it. Companies and countries vary in the degree that they accept various strategies we can use to fund time (e.g., house cleaners) or find time (e.g., vacations). Societies enforce different expectations on us, depending on our demographic characteristics and social class backgrounds. Women are expected to do more of the chores at home, and they believe they should pursue multiple goals at once, making high-status jobs seem less desirable and attainable for them than for men. People from lower income brackets are often expected to invest more in their families and work jobs that lack set schedules, forcing poorer people to choose between caring for the people they love or keeping the lights on.

For more research on how the causes and consequences of time poverty differs depending on social class and gender, see Hartmut Rosa, *Social Acceleration: A New Theory of Modernity* (New York: Columbia University Press, 2013). We also must make time-versus-money decisions in collaboration with our partners. This can be difficult. See H. R. Bowles and K. L. McGinn, "Gender in Job Negotiations: A Two-Level Game," *Negotiation Journal* 24, no. 4 (2008): 393–410, for strategies on how to navigate these choices.

While I have focused this book almost exclusively on decisions we make as individuals, choices about time and money do not happen in a vacuum. More research is needed to understand and intervene on the embedded nature of these values and actions.

## Does My Location Shape the Happiness Value of Time?

I'm often asked whether valuing time is more predictive of happiness for people who live in areas that are less work obsessed. As you might have guessed, the answer is yes. My colleagues and I looked at the question of how work norms and work beliefs shape the ways people spend their time and their enjoyment of leisure time. People who lived in places in the United States where their peers worked a lot of hours felt less happy when they engaged in leisure activities such as socializing and volunteering. Beliefs about work also mattered. If they lived in places where people believed that hard work was a critical part of what it meant to be a good person, our respondents also enjoyed leisure less, no matter how many hours their peers worked.

Together, these findings tell us that the way our peers act, and the values that are espoused in our society about the value of work, can play an important role in determining whether our time-smart decisions will pay off for personal happiness. To reap the joy of making time-first decisions, we need to encourage entire societies to value time, too.

## Why Can't You Just Tell Me What to Do?

I am often asked to provide a personalized formula for attaining time affluence and happiness. On this point, I am a source of perpetual disappointment. There is no one-size-fits-all solution. We all have different values, needs, and priorities. And we all respond differently to time choices.

Here's a personal example. Inspired by the research underlying this book, my partner recently decided to quit his full-time job. He now works as a freelancer, and he chooses when and where to work. This schedule control has, he says, "dramatically" reduced his stress. He loves feeling like his own boss. Yet one person's bliss is another's hell. Some people would pay *not* to have flexibility. See A. Mas and A. Pallais, "Valuing Alternative Work Arrangements," *American Economic Review* 107, no. 12 (2017): 3722–3759. Other people are so busy that they want to hire a house cleaner, but they don't, because they are trying to teach their kids the value of hard work. This decision is fine, too.

In short, the path to time affluence will not look the same for everyone. My best advice is to incorporate the approaches from this book that resonate the most—and then learn by trial and error. Infuse your day-to-day and major life decisions with time-smart strategies such as funding time, finding time, and framing time. For fun, try the activities that you are most resistant to.

If you hate the idea of hiring someone to clean your house or do your laundry, try it once, and see whether you still hate it. If you do, reflect on the reasons. You will learn the most if you actively push yourself out of your comfort zone every once in a while. This is generally true about money, time, and life.

Then tell me what solutions you liked and which ones you didn't. What worked? What was a waste of time? What did your partner think? We can work together to experiment with, and co-create, solutions for time poverty. Put the following Time-Affluence Checklist on your fridge as a reminder to experiment and have fun.

# Time-Affluence Checklist

If you are feeling time stressed, do the following:

✓ **Track your time.** Determine where your hours are going.

✓ **Think about what you enjoy doing.** Focus more on what makes you happy, what brings you meaning, or what is productive.

✓ **Find small pockets of free time to do more of these activities.** Prioritize the feelings that you want more of (e.g., pleasure, meaning, productivity).

✓ **Think about what you do not enjoy or what brings you stress.** Focus on what brings you misery or stress, or what is unproductive.

✓ **Reduce the amount of time you spend engaging in these experiences.** Minimize these experiences by funding time (e.g., outsourcing), finding time (e.g., canceling meetings), or reframing time (e.g., focusing on the positive).

✓ **Block out the free hours you have found for yourself.** Schedule the activities you want to do during your free time. If you want to spend more time reading, block out exactly when you are going to do this.

✓ **Enjoy your leisure.** After going through all this effort, turn off your work email and enjoy yourself. You deserve it.

# NOTES

For a more comprehensive description of these citations and the ways they relate to the research I have cited in this book, see awhillans.com.

## Introduction

1. For a review linking time famine to negative outcomes, see L. Giurge and A. V. Whillans, "Beyond Material Poverty: Why Time Poverty Matters for Individuals, Organisations, and Nations" (working paper, Harvard Business School, no. 20-051, 2020).

2. My research documents a link between time orientation (as measured by the Taylor-versus-Morgan question) and well-being, work hours, volunteering, and daily time-use decisions. A. V. Whillans, A. C. Weidman, and E. W. Dunn, "Valuing Time over Money Is Associated with Greater Happiness," *Social Psychological and Personality Science* 7, no. 3 (2016): 213–222.

3. Whillans et al., "Valuing Time over Money Is Associated with Greater Happiness." See also J. F. Helliwell and R. D. Putnam, "The Social Context of Well-Being," *Philosophical Transactions of the Royal Society of London, Series B: Biological Sciences* 359 (2004): 1435–1446.

4. A. V. Whillans and E. W. Dunn, "Valuing Time over Money Is Associated with Greater Social Connection," *Journal of Social and Personal Relationships* 36, no. 8 (2019): 2549–2565.

5. G. M. Sandstrom and E. W. Dunn, "Social Interactions and Well-Being: The Surprising Power of Weak Ties," *Personality and Social Psychology Bulletin* 40, no. 7 (2014): 910–922.

6. A. V. Whillans, J. Pow, and M. I. Norton, "Buying Time Promotes Relationship Satisfaction" (working paper, Harvard Business School, no. 18-072, January 2020).

7. A. Whillans, L. Macchia, and E. Dunn, "Valuing Time over Money Predicts Happiness after a Major Life Transition: A Preregistered Longitudinal Study of Graduating Students," *Science Advances* 5, no. 9 (2019): eaax2615. For a review, see E. W. Dunn, A. V. Whillans, M. I. Norton, and L. B. Aknin, "Prosocial Spending and Buying Time: Money As a Tool for Increasing Well-Being," *Advances in Experimental Social Psychology* 61 (2019): 67–126.

8. A. V. Whillans, A. Lee-Yoon, and E. W. Dunn, "When Guilt Undermines Consumer Willingness to Buy Time" (working paper, Harvard Business School, no. 18-057, January 2018, revised January 2020).

9. Giurge and Whillans, "Beyond Material Poverty." See also I. Hirway, *Mainstreaming Unpaid Work: Time-Use Data in Developing Policies* (Oxford: Oxford University Press, 2017).

10. J. M. Darley and C. D. Batson, "'From Jerusalem to Jericho': A Study of Situational and Dispositional Variables in Helping Behavior," *Journal of Personality and Social Psychology* 27, no. 1 (1973): 100.

11. Whillans et al., "Valuing Time over Money Is Associated with Greater Happiness." See also A. C. Hafenbrack, L. D. Cameron, G. M. Spreitzer, C. Zhang, L. J. Noval, and S. Shaffakat, "Helping People by Being in the Present: Mindfulness Increases Prosocial Behavior," *Organizational Behavior and Human Decision Processes* (2019).

12. A. V. Whillans and E. W. Dunn, "Thinking About Time As Money Decreases Environmental Behavior," *Organizational Behavior and Human Decision Processes* 127 (2015): 44–52.

13. A. V. Whillans, "Time for Happiness: Why the Pursuit of Money Isn't Bringing You Joy—And What Will," hbr.org, January 29, 2019, https://www.hbs.edu/faculty/Pages/item.aspx?num=55600.

## Chapter 1

1. A. V. Whillans, "Time for Happiness: Why the Pursuit of Money Isn't Bringing You Joy—And What Will," hbr.org, January 29, 2019, https://www.hbs.edu/faculty/Pages/item.aspx?num=55600.

2. D. S. Hamermesh and J. Lee, "Stressed Out on Four Continents: Time Crunch or Yuppie Kvetch?" *Review of Economics and Statistics* 89, no. 2 (2007): 374–383. See also D. S. Hamermesh, "Not Enough Time?" *American Economist* 59, no. 2 (2014): 119–127.

3. K. Parker and W. Wang, *Modern Parenthood: Roles of Moms and Dads Converge As They Balance Work and Family* (Washington, DC: Pew Research Center, March 14, 2013), https://www.pewsocialtrends.org/wp-content/uploads/sites/3/2013/03/FINAL_modern_parenthood_03-2013.pdf.

4. Pew Research Center, "Raising Kids and Running a Household: How Working Parents Share the Load," November 4, 2015, https://www.pewsocialtrends.org/2015/11/04/raising-kids-and-running-a-household-how-working-parents-share-the-load/.

5. T. Kasser and K. M. Sheldon, "Time Affluence as a Path Toward Personal Happiness and Ethical Business Practice: Empirical Evidence from Four Studies," *Journal of Business Ethics* 84, no. 2 (2009): 243–255. See also Whillans, "Time for Happiness."

6. C. Mogilner, A. Whillans, and M. I. Norton, "Time, Money, and Subjective Well-Being," in *Handbook of Well-Being, Noba Scholar Handbook Series: Subjective Well-Being*, eds. E. Diener, S. Oishi, and L. Tay (Salt Lake City, UT: DEF Publishers, 2018).

7. S. Roxburgh, "'There Just Aren't Enough Hours in the Day': The Mental Health Consequences of Time Pressure," *Journal of Health and Social Behavior* 45, no. 2 (2004): 115–131; J. Jabs and C. M. Devine, "Time Scarcity and Food Choices: An Overview," *Appetite* 47, no. 2 (2006): 196–204; D. Venn and L. Strazdins, "Your Money or Your Time? How Both Types of Scarcity Matter to Physical Activity and Healthy Eating," *Social Science and Medicine* 172 (2017): 98–106; J. De Graaf, ed., *Take Back Your Time: Fighting Overwork and Time Poverty in America* (San Francisco: Berrett-Koehler, 2003).

8. Gallup estimates the cost of stress to be about $190 billion per year in the United States as of 2013. Gallup, "Report: State of the American Workplace," September 22, 2013, https://www.gallup.com/services/176708/state-american-workplace.aspx. The estimated cost of stress on the US health care system is estimated at 5 percent to 8 percent of total health care spending each year: J. Goh, J. Pfeffer, and S. A. Zenios, "The Relationship Between Workplace Stressors and Mortality and Health Costs in the United States," *Management Science* 62, no. 2 (2015): 608–628.

9. W. F. Stewart, J. A. Ricci, E. Chee, S. R. Hahn, and D. Morganstein, "Cost of Lost Productive Work Time Among US Workers with Depression," *JAMA* 289, no. 23 (2003): 3135–3144.

10. P. E. Greenberg, A. A. Fournier, T. Sisitsky, C. T. Pike, and R. C. Kessler, "The Economic Burden of Adults with Major Depressive Disorder in the US," *Journal of Clinical Psychiatry* 76, no. 2 (2015): 155–162.

11. L. A. Perlow, "The Time Famine: Toward a Sociology of Work Time," *Administrative Science Quarterly* 44, no. 1 (1999): 57–81.

12. M. Aguiar and E. Hurst, "Measuring Trends in Leisure: The Allocation of Time Over Five Decades," *Quarterly Journal of Economics* 122, no. 3 (2007): 969–1006.

13. The OECD finds that full-time employees in the United States worked an average of 37.8 hours per week in 1950. In contrast, in 2017, they worked an average of 34.2 hours per week. J. C. Messenger, S. Lee, and D. McCann, *Working Time around the World: Trends in Working Hours, Laws, and Policies in a Global Comparative Perspective* (Oxfordshire, UK: Routledge, 2007).

14. In a 2015 Pew survey, seven in ten Americans reported using online or sharing economy services. A. Smith, "How Americans Define the Sharing Economy," Pew Research Center, May 20, 2016, https://www.pewresearch.org/fact-tank/2016/05/20/how-americans-define-the-sharing-economy/.

15. In the United States, adults spend an average of three hours and twenty minutes each day using their smart phones—double the amount five years ago. R. Marvin, "Tech Addiction by the Numbers: How Much Time We Spend Online," *PC Magazine*, June 11, 2018, https://www.pcmag.com/article/361587/tech-addiction-by-the-numbers-how-much-time-we-spend-online.

16. Americans check their phones about once every twelve minutes. SWNS, "Americans Check Their Phones 80 Times a Day: Study," *New York Post*, November 8, 2017, https://nypost.com/2017/11/08/americans-check-their-phones-80-times-a-day-study/.

17. A. Bellezza, N. Paharia, and A. Keinan, "Conspicuous Consumption of Time: When Busyness and Lack of Leisure Time Become a Status Symbol," *Journal of Consumer Research* 44, no. 1 (2016): 118–138.

18. L. E. Park, D. E. Ward, and K. Naragon-Gainey, "It's All About the Money (For Some): Consequences of Financially Contingent Self-Worth," *Personality and Social Psychology Bulletin* 43, no. 5 (2017): 601–622.

19. M. Mazmanian, W. J. Orlikowski, and J. Yates, "The Autonomy Paradox: The Implications of Mobile Email Devices for Knowledge Professionals," *Organization Science* 24, no. 5 (2013): 1337–1357.

20. R. J. Dwyer, K. Kushlev, and E. W. Dunn, "Smartphone Use Undermines Enjoyment of Face-to-Face Social Interactions," *Journal of Experimental Social Psychology* 78 (2018): 233–239; K. Kushlev and E. W. Dunn, "Smartphones Distract Parents from Cultivating Feelings of Connection When Spending Time with Their Children," *Journal of Social and Personal Relationships* 36, no. 6 (2019): 1619–1639; and K. Kushlev, R. Dwyer, and E. W. Dunn, "The Social Price of Constant Connectivity: Smartphones Impose Subtle Costs on Well-Being," *Current Directions in Psychological Science* (2019).

21. The term *time confetti* was popularized by Brigid Schulte in *Overwhelmed: How to Work, Love, and Play When No One Has the Time* (New York: Picador, 2014). See also S. E. Lindley, "Making Time," in *Proceedings of the 18th ACM Conference on Computer Supported Cooperative Work and Social Computing* (ACM, February 2015): 1442–1452.

22. J. M. Hudson, J. Christensen, W. A. Kellogg, and T. Erickson, "I'd Be Overwhelmed, but It's Just One More Thing to Do: Availability and Interruption in Research Management," in *Proceedings of the SIGCHI Conference on Human Factors in Computing Systems*, eds. R. Grinter et al. (New York: Association for Computing Machinery, 2006), 97–104; B. O'Conaill and D. Frohlich, "Timespace in the Workplace: Dealing

with Interruptions," in *Conference Companion on Human Factors in Computing Systems*, ed. C. Plaisant (New York: Association for Computing Machinery, 1994).

23. Time poverty is caused in part by how well activities fit together in our minds. When we feel that we are trying to complete two conflicting activities (e.g., taking care of our kid *and* checking work email), these conflicting goals can increase feelings of time stress. J. Etkin, I. Evangelidis, and J. Aaker, "Pressed for Time? Goal Conflict Shapes How Time Is Perceived, Spent, and Valued," *Journal of Marketing Research* 52, no. 3 (2015): 394–406. It is worth noting that some research finds that interruptions, such as commercial breaks, increase our enjoyment of hedonic experiences such as watching funny TV shows. See L. D. Nelson and T. Meyvis, "Interrupted Consumption: Adaptation and the Disruption of Hedonic Experience," *Journal of Marketing Research* 45, no. 6 (2008): 654–664; and L. D. Nelson, T. Meyvis, and J. Galak, "Enhancing the Television-Viewing Experience Through Commercial Interruptions," *Journal of Consumer Research* 36, no. 2 (2009): 160–172. However, these studies typically involve *passive* interruptions that do not demand active attention (i.e., commercial breaks) and do not remind us of the productivity costs of engaging in the current leisure activity (i.e., watching TV).

24. This fact is derived from a survey of 600 working Americans recruited through a private consulting firm. David Kelleher, "Survey: 81% of US Employees Check Their Work Mail Outside Work Hours," *TechTalk*, May 20, 2013, https://techtalk.gfi.com/survey -81-of-u-s-employees-check-their-work-mail-outside-work-hours/.

25. Multitasking is stressful because it creates "attention residue." It takes time to recover from shifting our minds away from the present, to another activity, and back to the present. S. Leroy, "Why Is It So Hard to Do My Work? The Challenge of Attention Residue When Switching Between Work Tasks," *Organizational Behavior and Human Decision Processes* 109, no. 2 (2009): 168–181. Experiences of attention residue in task switching depend on the tasks we are switching between and how we think about them. S. Leroy and A. M. Schmidt, "The Effect of Regulatory Focus on Attention Residue and Performance During Interruptions," *Organizational Behavior and Human Decision Processes* 137 (2016): 218–235.

26. G. N. Tonietto, S. A. Malkoc, and S. M. Nowlis, "When an Hour Feels Shorter: Future Boundary Tasks Alter Consumption by Contracting Time," *Journal of Consumer Research* 45, no. 5 (2019): 1085–1102.

27. E. W. Dunn, A. V. Whillans, M. I. Norton, and L. B. Aknin, "Prosocial Spending and Buying Time: Money As a Tool for Increasing Well-Being," *Advances in Experimental Social Psychology* 61 (2020): 67–126.

28. G. E. Donnelly, T. Zheng, E. Haisley, and M. I. Norton, "The Amount and Source of Millionaires' Wealth (Moderately) Predicts Their Happiness," *Personality and Social Psychology Bulletin* 44, no. 5 (2018): 684–699.

29. K. Kushlev, E. W. Dunn, and R. E. Lucas, "Higher Income Is Associated with Less Daily Sadness but Not More Daily Happiness," *Social Psychological and Personality Science* 6, no. 5 (2015): 483–489; and N. W. Hudson, R. E. Lucas, M. B. Donnellan, and K. Kushlev, "Income Reliably Predicts Daily Sadness, but Not Happiness: A Replication and Extension of Kushlev, Dunn, & Lucas (2015)," *Social Psychological and Personality Science* 7, no. 8 (2016): 828–836.

30. A. T. Jebb, L. Tay, E. Diener, and S. Oishi, "Happiness, Income Satiation and Turning Points around the World," *Nature Human Behaviour* 2, no. 1 (2018): 33.

31. J. W. Zhang, R. T. Howell, and C. J. Howell, "Living in Wealthy Neighborhoods Increases Material Desires and Maladaptive Consumption," *Journal of Consumer Culture* 16, no. 1 (2016): 297–316; and H. Kim, M. J. Callan, A. I. Gheorghiu, and W. J. Matthews, "Social Comparison, Personal Relative Deprivation, and Materialism," *British Journal of Social Psychology* 56, no. 2 (2017): 373–392.

32. P. M. Ruberton, J. Gladstone, and S. Lyubomirsky, "How Your Bank Balance Buys Happiness: The Importance of 'Cash on Hand' to Life Satisfaction," *Emotion* 16, no. 5 (2016): 575.

33. L. B. Aknin, M. I. Norton, and E. W. Dunn, "From Wealth to Well-Being? Money Matters, but Less Than People Think," *Journal of Positive Psychology* 4, no. 6 (2009): 523–527.

34. D. Kahneman, A. B. Krueger, D. Schkade, N. Schwarz, and A. A. Stone, "Would You Be Happier If You Were Richer? A Focusing Illusion," *Science* 312, no. 5782 (2006): 1908–1910.

35. Hamermesh and Lee, "Stressed Out on Four Continents: Time Crunch or Yuppie Kvetch?"

36. S. E. DeVoe and J. Pfeffer, "Time Is Tight: How Higher Economic Value of Time Increases Feelings of Time Pressure," *Journal of Applied Psychology* 96, no. 4 (2011): 665.

37. Ibid.

38. A. Furnham, M. Bond, P. Heaven, D. Hilton, T. Lobel, J. Masters, and H. Van Daalen, "A Comparison of Protestant Work Ethic Beliefs in Thirteen Nations," *Journal of Social Psychology* 133, no. 2 (1993): 185–197. In light of strong Protestant work ethic beliefs in the United States (historically and present-day), in the United States busyness is seen as a status symbol. For example, people who announce that they are very busy are granted higher social standing in the United States and are seen as wealthier and more important than people who announce that they have a lot of leisure time available. See Bellezza et al., "Conspicuous Consumption of Time: When Busyness and Lack of Leisure Time Become a Status Symbol." This effect holds only in the United States and not in Europe.

39. J. D. Hur and L. F. Nordgren, "Paying for Performance: Performance Incentives Increase Desire for the Reward Object," *Journal of Personality and Social Psychology* 111, no. 3 (2016): 301.

40. I. Dar-Nimrod, C. D. Rawn, D. R. Lehman, and B. Schwartz, "The Maximization Paradox: The Costs of Seeking Alternatives," *Personality and Individual Differences* 46, no. 495-6 (2009): 631–635; and S. I. Rick, C. E. Cryder, and G. Loewenstein, "Tightwads and Spendthrifts," *Journal of Consumer Research* 34, no. 6 (2008): 767–782.

41. Working parents with young children are time stressed: H. Buddelmeyer, D. S. Hamermesh, and M. Wooden, "The Stress Cost of Children on Moms and Dads," *European Economic Review* 109 (2018): 148–161; L. Craig and J. E. Brown, "Feeling Rushed: Gendered Time Quality, Work Hours, Nonstandard Work Schedules, and Spousal Crossover," *Journal of Marriage and Family* 79, no. 1 (2017): 225–242. Even busy working parents report they would rather have more money than more time: A. V. Whillans, A. C. Weidman, and E. W. Dunn, "Valuing Time over Money Is Associated with Greater Happiness," *Social Psychological and Personality Science* 7, no. 3 (2016): 213–222, study 4.

42. A. V. Whillans, E. W. Dunn, P. Smeets, R. Bekkers, and M. I. Norton, "Buying Time Promotes Happiness," *Proceedings of the National Academy of Sciences* 114, no. 32 (2017): 8523–8527, study 9.

43. Data: Open Science Framework, "Time Use and Happiness of Millionaires," June 16, 2016, https://osf.io/vndmt/. See also P. Smeets, A. Whillans, R. Bekkers, and M. I. Norton, "Time Use and Happiness of Millionaires: Evidence from the Netherlands," *Social Psychological and Personality Science* 11, no. 3. (2020): 295–307.

44. D. Soman, "The Mental Accounting of Sunk Time Costs: Why Time Is Not Like Money," *Journal of Behavioral Decision Making* 14, no. 3 (2001): 169–185.

45. Derek Thompson, a staff writer for *The Atlantic*, provided this quotation in a February 2019 article, "Workism Is Making Americans Miserable," https://www.theatlantic.com/ideas/archive/2019/02/religion-workism-making-americans-miserable/583441/.

46. J. M. Horowitz and N. Graf, "Most U.S. Teens See Anxiety and Depression as a Major Problem Among Their Peers," Pew Research Center, February 20, 2019, https://www.pewsocialtrends.org/2019/02/20/most-u-s-teens-see-anxiety-and-depression-as-a-major-problem-among-their-peers/.

47. For a review, see A. Keinan, S. Bellezza, and N. Paharia, "The Symbolic Value of Time," *Current Opinion in Psychology* 26 (2019): 58–61.

48. F. Solt, "The Standardized World Income Inequality Database," *Social Science Quarterly* 97, no. 5 (2016): 1267–1281.

49. P. K. Piff, M. W. Kraus, and D. Keltner, "Unpacking the Inequality Paradox: The Psychological Roots of Inequality and Social Class," *Advances in Experimental Social Psychology* 57 (2018): 53–124.

50. Whillans et al., "Valuing Time over Money Predicts Happiness after a Major Life Transition: A Preregistered Longitudinal Study of Graduating Students."

51. A. Whillans, "Exchanging Cents for Seconds: The Happiness Benefits of Choosing Time over Money" (doctoral dissertation, University of British Columbia, 2017), study 5, section 2.9.

52. J. C. Lee, D. L. Hall, and W. Wood, "Experiential or Material Purchases? Social Class Determines Purchase Happiness," *Psychological Science* 29, no. 7 (2018): 1031–1039; and A. Whillans, A. Lee-Yoon, and E. W. Dunn, "When Guilt Undermines Consumer Willingness to Buy Time" (working paper, Harvard Business School, no. 18-057, January 2018, revised January 2020), study 2.

53. L. Park, Y. Hun Jung, J. Shultz-lee, D. Ward, P. Piff, and A. V. Whillans, "Psychological Pathways Linking Income Inequality in Adolescence to Well-Being in Adulthood" (working paper).

54. Bellezza et al., "Conspicuous Consumption of Time: When Busyness and Lack of Leisure Time Become a Status Symbol"; C. K. Hsee, A. X. Yang, and L. Wang, "Idleness Aversion and the Need for Justifiable Busyness," *Psychological Science* 21, no. 7 (2010), 926–930; and C. K. Hsee, J. Zhang, C. F. Cai, and S. Zhang, "Overearning," *Psychological Science* 24, no. 6 (2013): 852–859. For a review, see A. X. Yang and C. K. Hsee, "Idleness Versus Busyness," *Current Opinion in Psychology* 26 (2019): 15–18.

55. Bellezza et al., "Conspicuous Consumption of Time: When Busyness and Lack of Leisure Time Become a Status Symbol."

56. T. D. Wilson, D. A. Reinhard, E. C. Westgate, D. T. Gilbert, N. Ellerbeck, C. Hahn, and A. Shaked, "Just Think: The Challenges of the Disengaged Mind," *Science* 345, no. 6192 (2014): 75–77.

57. N. Whitehead, "People Would Rather Be Electrically Shocked Than Left Alone with Their Thoughts," *Science*, July 3, 2014, https://www.sciencemag.org/news/2014/07/people-would-rather-be-electrically-shocked-left-alone-their-thoughts.

58. M. Haller, M. Hadler, and G. Kaup, "Leisure Time in Modern Societies: A New Source of Boredom and Stress?" *Social Indicators Research* 111, no. 2 (2013): 403–434.

59. For a review, see J. D. Creswell, "Mindfulness Interventions," *Annual Review of Psychology* 68 (2017): 491–516.

60. G. Zauberman and J. G. Lynch Jr., "Resource Slack and Propensity to Discount Delayed Investments of Time Versus Money," *Journal of Experimental Psychology: General* 134, no. 1 (2005): 23.

61. H. E. Hershfield, "The Self over Time," *Current Opinion in Psychology* 26 (2019): 72–75.

62. R. Buehler, D. Griffin, and M. Ross, "Exploring the 'Planning Fallacy': Why People Underestimate Their Task Completion Times," *Journal of Personality and Social Psychology* 67, no. 3 (1994): 366; and R. Buehler and D. Griffin, "Planning, Personality, and Prediction: The Role of Future Focus in Optimistic Time Predictions," *Organizational Behavior and Human Decision Processes* 92, no. 1-2 (2003): 80–90.

63. K. Wilcox, J. Laran, A. T. Stephen, and P. P. Zubcsek, "How Being Busy Can Increase Motivation and Reduce Task Completion Time," *Journal of Personality and Social Psychology* 110, no. 3 (2016): 371.

64. M. Zhu, Y. Yang, and C. K. Hsee, "The Mere Urgency Effect," *Journal of Consumer Research* 45, no. 3 (2018): 673–690.

65. Wilcox et al., "How Being Busy Can Increase Motivation and Reduce Task Completion Time."

## Chapter 2

1. Major life decisions can have profound and lasting changes for subjective well-being. For related research, see G. Marum, J. Clench-Aas, R. B. Nes, and R. K. Raanaas, "The Relationship Between Negative Life Events, Psychological Distress and Life Satisfaction: A Population-Based Study," *Quality of Life Research* 23, no. 2 (2014): 601–611.

2. A. V. Whillans, A. C. Weidman, and E. W. Dunn, "Valuing Time over Money Is Associated with Greater Happiness," *Social Psychological and Personality Science* 7, no. 3 (2016): 213–222.

3. S. M. Tully and E. Sharma, "Context-Dependent Drivers of Discretionary Debt Decisions: Explaining Willingness to Borrow for Experiential Purchases," *Journal of Consumer Research* 44, no. 5 (2017): 960–973; S. M. Tully, H. E. Hershfield, and T. Meyvis, "Seeking Lasting Enjoyment with Limited Money: Financial Constraints Increase Preference for Material Goods over Experiences," *Journal of Consumer Research* 42, no. 1 (2015): 59–75; and L. E. Park, D. E. Ward, and K. Naragon-Gainey, "It's All About the Money (For Some): Consequences of Financially Contingent Self-Worth," *Personality and Social Psychology Bulletin* 43, no. 5 (2017): 601–622.

4. S. C. Matz, J. J. Gladstone, and D. Stillwell, "Money Buys Happiness When Spending Fits Our Personality," *Psychological Science* 27, no. 5 (2016): 715–725; and J. C. Lee, D. L. Hall, and W. Wood, "Experiential or Material Purchases? Social Class Determines Purchase Happiness," *Psychological Science* 29, no. 7 (2018): 1031–1039.

5. E. W. Dunn, A. V. Whillans, M. I. Norton, and L. B. Aknin, "Prosocial Spending and Buying Time: Money As a Tool for Increasing Well-Being," *Advances in Experimental Social Psychology* 61 (2020): 67–126.

6. L. I. Catalino and B. L. Fredrickson, "A Tuesday in the Life of a Flourisher: The Role of Positive Emotional Reactivity in Optimal Mental Health," *Emotion* 11, no. 4 (2011): 938.

7. C. Young and C. Lim, "Time As a Network Good: Evidence from Unemployment and the Standard Workweek," *Sociological Science* 1 (2014): 10.

8. M. P. White and P. Dolan, "Accounting for the Richness of Daily Activities," *Psychological Science* 20, no. 8 (2009): 1000–1008.

9. S. K. Nelson, K. Kushlev, and S. Lyubomirsky, "The Pains and Pleasures of Parenting: When, Why, and How Is Parenthood Associated with More or Less Well-Being?" *Psychological Bulletin* 140, no. 3 (2014): 846.

10. T. Burchardt, "Time, Income and Substantive Freedom: A Capability Approach," *Time and Society* 19, no. 3 (2010): 318–344.

11. R. E. Goodin, J. M. Rice, M. Bittman, and P. Saunders, "The Time-Pressure Illusion: Discretionary vs. Free Time," *Social Indicators Research* 73, no. 1 (2005): 43–70; and R. E. Goodin, J. M. Rice, A. Parpo, and L. Eriksson, *Discretionary Time: A New Measure of Freedom* (Cambridge: Cambridge University Press, 2008).

12. For reviews looking at when, whether, and how simple actions can result in lasting changes in well-being, see S. Lyubomirsky and K. Layous, "How Do Simple Positive Activities Increase Well-Being?" *Current Directions in Psychological Science* 22, no. 1 (2013): 57–62; and K. Layous and S. Lyubomirsky, "The How, Who, What, When, and Why of Happiness: Mechanisms Underlying the Success of Positive Interventions," in *Light and Dark Side of Positive Emotion*, ed. J. Gruber and J. Moskowitz (Oxford: Oxford University Press, in press).

13. D. Kahneman and A. B. Krueger, "Developments in the Measurement of Subjective Well-Being," *Journal of Economic Perspectives* 20, no. 1 (2006): 3–24; A. B. Krueger, D. Kahneman, D. Schkade, N. Schwarz, and A. A. Stone, "National Time Accounting: The Currency of Life," in *Measuring the Subjective Well-Being of Nations: National Accounts of Time Use and Well-Being*, ed. A. B. Krueger (Chicago: University of Chicago Press, 2009), 9–86; and A. A. Stone and C. Mackie, National Academies of Sciences, Engineering, and

Medicine, "The Subjective Well-Being Module of the American Time Use Survey: Assessment for Its Continuation," in *Subjective Well-Being: Measuring Happiness, Suffering, and Other Dimensions of Experience* (Washington, DC: National Academies Press, 2013).

14. A. Mani, S. Mullainathan, E. Shafir, and J. Zhao, "Poverty Impedes Cognitive Function," *Science* 341, no. 6149 (2013): 976–980; S. Mullainathan and E. Shafir, *Scarcity: Why Having Too Little Means So Much* (New York: Macmillan, 2013); G. V. Pepper and D. Nettle, "Strengths, Altered Investment, Risk Management, and Other Elaborations on the Behavioural Constellation of Deprivation," *Behavioral and Brain Sciences* 40 (2017); and A. K. Shah, S. Mullainathan, and E. Shafir, "Some Consequences of Having Too Little," *Science* 338, no. 6107 (2012): 682–685.

15. C. Roux, K. Goldsmith, and A. Bonezzi, "On the Psychology of Scarcity: When Reminders of Resource Scarcity Promote Selfish (and Generous) Behavior," *Journal of Consumer Research* 42, no. 4 (2015): 615–631; and Tully et al., "Seeking Lasting Enjoyment with Limited Money: Financial Constraints Increase Preference for Material Goods over Experiences."

16. E. L. Kelly and P. Moen, "Rethinking the Clockwork of Work: Why Schedule Control May Pay Off at Work and at Home," *Advances in Developing Human Resources* 9, no. 4 (2007): 487–506; E. L. Kelly, P. Moen, and E. Tranby, "Changing Workplaces to Reduce Work-Family Conflict: Schedule Control in a White-Collar Organization," *American Sociological Review* 76, no. 2 (2011): 265–290; P. Moen, E. L. Kelly, E. Tranby, and Q. Huang, "Changing Work, Changing Health: Can Real Work-Time Flexibility Promote Health Behaviors and Well-Being?" *Journal of Health and Social Behavior* 52, no. 4 (2011): 404–429; and P. Moen, E. L. Kelly, and R. Hill, "Does Enhancing Work-Time Control and Flexibility Reduce Turnover? A Naturally Occurring Experiment," *Social Problems* 58, no. 1 (2011): 69–98.

17. For a review, see E. E. Kossek, L. B. Hammer, E. L. Kelly, and P. Moen, "Designing Work, Family & Health Organizational Change Initiatives," *Organizational Dynamics* 43, no. 1 (2014): 53.

18. P. Smeets, A. Whillans, R. Bekkers, and M. I. Norton, "Time Use and Happiness of Millionaires: Evidence from the Netherlands," *Social Psychological and Personality Science* 11, no. 3. (2020): 295–307.

19. N. Lathia, G. M. Sandstrom, C. Mascolo, and P. J. Rentfrow, "Happier People Live More Active Lives: Using Smartphones to Link Happiness and Physical Activity," *PLOS ONE* 12, no. 1 (2017).

20. Smeets et al., "Time Use and Happiness of Millionaires: Evidence from the Netherlands"; for a review, see Mogilner et al., "Time, Money, and Subjective Well-Being."

21. Data available upon request.

22. B. Schwartz, A. Ward, J. Monterosso, S. Lyubomirsky, K. White, and D. R. Lehman, "Maximizing Versus Satisficing: Happiness Is a Matter of Choice," *Journal of Personality and Social Psychology* 83, no. 5 (2002): 1178.

23. J. Holt-Lunstad, T. B. Smith, M. Baker, T. Harris, and D. Stephenson, "Loneliness and Social Isolation As Risk Factors for Mortality: A Meta-Analytic Review," *Perspectives on Psychological Science* 10, no. 2 (2015): 227–237.

24. G. M. Sandstrom and E. W. Dunn, "Social Interactions and Well-Being: The Surprising Power of Weak Ties," *Personality and Social Psychology Bulletin* 40, no. 7 (2014): 910–922; G. M. Sandstrom and E. W. Dunn, "Is Efficiency Overrated? Minimal Social Interactions Lead to Belonging and Positive Affect," *Social Psychological and Personality Science* 5, no. 4 (2014): 437–442; N. Epley and J. Schroeder, "Mistakenly Seeking Solitude," *Journal of Experimental Psychology: General* 143, no. 5 (2014): 1980; and E. J. Boothby, G. Cooney, G. M. Sandstrom, and M. S. Clark, "The Liking Gap in Conversations: Do People Like Us More Than We Think?" *Psychological Science* 29, no. 11 (2018): 1742–1756.

25. C. Mogilner, Z. Chance, and M. I. Norton, "Giving Time Gives You Time," *Psychological Science* 23, no. 10 (2012): 1233–1238; and Z. Chance and M. I. Norton, "I Give

Therefore I Have: Charitable Giving and Subjective Wealth," paper presented at the Association for Consumer Research Annual North American Conference, Jacksonville, FL, October 1, 2010. When we see ourselves giving away valuable resources (such as time and money), it sends a signal to ourselves that we must have enough of both of these resources. This is known as *self-perception theory*: D. J. Bem, "Self-Perception Theory," *Advances in Experimental Social Psychology* 6 (1972): 1–62.

26. M. Rudd, K. D. Vohs, and J. Aaker, "Awe Expands People's Perception of Time, Alters Decision Making, and Enhances Well-Being," *Psychological Science* 23, no. 10 (2012): 1130–1136.

27. D. Keltner and J. Haidt, "Approaching Awe, a Moral, Spiritual, and Aesthetic Emotion," *Cognition and Emotion* 17 (2003): 297–314; P. K. Piff, P. Dietze, M. Feinberg, D. M. Stancato, and D. Keltner, "Awe, the Small Self, and Prosocial Behavior," *Journal of Personality and Social Psychology* 108, no. 6 (2015): 883; J. W. Zhang, P. K. Piff, R. Iyer, S. Koleva, and D. Keltner, "An Occasion for Unselfing: Beautiful Nature Leads to Prosociality," *Journal of Environmental Psychology* 37 (2014): 61–72.

28. M. E. Porter and N. Nohria, "How CEOs Manage Time," *Harvard Business Review*, July–August 2018.

29. Dunn et al., "Prosocial Spending and Buying Time: Money As a Tool for Increasing Well-Being."

30. S. Frederick, N. Novemsky, J. Wang, R. Dhar, and S. Nowlis, "Opportunity Cost Neglect," *Journal of Consumer Research* 36, no. 4 (2009): 553–561; and M. Gagne and A. Whillans, "Overcoming Barriers to Buying Happier Time," *Undergraduate Journal of Psychology* 75 (2016). Data available upon request.

31. A. V. Whillans, "Time for Happiness: Why the Pursuit of Money Isn't Bringing You Joy—And What Will," Special issues on HBR Big Idea: Time Poor and Unhappy, hbr.org, January 29, 2019, https://www.hbs.edu/faculty/Pages/item.aspx?num=55600.

32. Whillans, "Time for Happiness."

33. Whillans, "Time for Happiness."

34. The participant was recruited through online data collection conducted in collaboration with the *New York Times*. *NYT* gave me permission to use the data collected as part of an article it published, as long as we masked participants' names and any identifying information. C. Richards, "Maybe You Shouldn't Outsource Everything After All," May 7, 2018, https://www.nytimes.com/2018/05/07/your-money/outsource -happiness.html.

35. A. V. Whillans and C. West, "Alleviating Time Poverty Among the Working Poor" (working paper, Harvard Business School, 2020), https://www.aeaweb.org/conference /2020/preliminary/paper/3rf3SEb2.

36. A. V. Whillans and E. W. Dunn, "When Guilt Undermines Consumer Willingness to Buy Time" (working paper, Harvard Business School, no. 18-057, January 2018, revised January 2020), study 2.

37. A. Lee-Yoon, G. Donnelly, and A. V. Whillans, "Overcoming Resource Scarcity: Consumers' Responses to Gifts Intending to Save Time and Money" (working paper, Harvard Business School, no. 20-072, 2020).

38. The participant was recruited through online data collection conducted in collaboration with the *New York Times*. *NYT* gave me permission to use the data collected as part of an article it published, as long as participants' names and any identifying information was masked. C. Richards, "Maybe You Shouldn't Outsource Everything After All," May 7, 2018, https://www.nytimes.com/2018/05/07/your-money/outsource -happiness.html.

39. A. V. Whillans, J. Pow, and M. I. Norton, "Buying Time Promotes Relationship Satisfaction" (working paper, Harvard Business School, no. 18-072, January 2020); and M. S. Clark and J. Mils, "The Difference Between Communal and Exchange Relationships: What It Is and Is Not," *Personality and Social Psychology Bulletin* 19, no. 6 (1993): 684–691.

40. Lee-Yoon et al., "Overcoming Resource Scarcity: Consumers' Responses to Gifts Intending to Save Time and Money."

41. J. Galak, J. Givi, and E. F. Williams, "Why Certain Gifts Are Great to Give but Not to Get: A Framework for Understanding Errors in Gift Giving," *Current Directions in Psychological Science* 25, no. 6 (2016): 380–385.

42. P. E. Jose, B. T. Lim, and F. B. Bryant, "Does Savoring Increase Happiness? A Daily Diary Study," *Journal of Positive Psychology* 7, no. 3 (2012): 176–187; and J. Quoidbach, E. V. Berry, M. Hansenne, and M. Mikolajczak, "Positive Emotion Regulation and Well-Being: Comparing the Impact of Eight Savoring and Dampening Strategies," *Personality and Individual Differences* 49, no. 5 (2010): 368–373.

43. C. West, C. Mogilner, and S. DeVoe, "Taking Vacation Increases Meaning at Work," *ACR North American Advances* (2017). For a review, see C. Mogilner, H. E. Hershfield, and J. Aaker, "Rethinking Time: Implications for Well-Being," *Consumer Psychology Review* 1, no. 1 (2018): 41–53.

44. J. Etkin, I. Evangelidis, and J. Aaker, "Pressed for Time? Goal Conflict Shapes How Time Is Perceived, Spent, and Valued," *Journal of Marketing Research* 52, no. 3 (2015): 394–406.

45. A. J. Crum, P. Salovey, and S. Achor, "Rethinking Stress: The Role of Mindsets in Determining the Stress Response," *Journal of Personality and Social Psychology* 104, no. 4 (2013): 716; and O. H. Zahrt and A. J. Crum, "Perceived Physical Activity and Mortality: Evidence from Three Nationally Representative US Samples," *Health Psychology* 36, no. 11 (2017): 1017.

46. Crum et al., "Rethinking Stress: The Role of Mindsets in Determining the Stress Response."

47. J. Jachimowicz, J. Lee, B. R. Staats, J. Menges, and F. Gino, "Between Home and Work: Commuting As an Opportunity for Role Transitions" (working paper, Harvard Business School NOM Unit, no. 16-077, 2019).

48. L. L. Carstensen, "Selectivity Theory: Social Activity in Life-Span Context," *Annual Review of Gerontology and Geriatrics* 11, no. 1 (1991): 195–217; L. L. Carstensen, "Social and Emotional Patterns in Adulthood: Support for Socioemotional Selectivity Theory," *Psychology and Aging* 7, no. 3 (1992): 331; and L. L. Carstensen, "Evidence for a Life-Span Theory of Socioemotional Selectivity," *Current Directions in Psychological Science* 4, no. 5 (1995): 151–156.

49. A. Bhattacharjee and C. Mogilner, "Happiness from Ordinary and Extraordinary Experiences," *Journal of Consumer Research* 41, no. 1 (2013): 1–17.

50. J. L. Kurtz, "Looking to the Future to Appreciate the Present: The Benefits of Perceived Temporal Scarcity," *Psychological Science* 19, no. 12 (2008): 1238–1241; and K. Layous, J. Kurtz, J. Chancellor, and S. Lyubomirsky, "Reframing the Ordinary: Imagining Time As Scarce Increases Well-Being," *Journal of Positive Psychology* 13, no. 3 (2018): 301–308.

51. J. Quoidbach and E. W. Dunn, "Give It Up: A Strategy for Combating Hedonic Adaptation," *Social Psychological and Personality Science* 4, no. 5 (2013): 563–568.

52. Underlying data available upon request.

53. R. A. Emmons and C. M. Shelton, "Gratitude and the Science of Positive Psychology," *Handbook of Positive Psychology* 18 (2002): 459–471; and J. W. Pennebaker, "Writing About Emotional Experiences As a Therapeutic Process," *Psychological Science* 8, no. 3 (1997): 162–166.

54. M. Li and S. DeVoe, "Putting Off Balance for Later: A Temporal Construal Approach to Time Allocation" (working paper, UCLA School of Management, 2020).

55. E. T. Higgins, "Value from Regulatory Fit," *Current Directions in Psychological Science* 14, no. 4 (2005): 209–213; and J. Cesario, H. Grant, and E. T. Higgins, "Regulatory Fit and Persuasion: Transfer from 'Feeling Right,'" *Journal of Personality and Social Psychology* 86, no. 3 (2004): 388.

56. Whillans et al., "Valuing Time over Money Is Associated with Greater Happiness."

57. Adapted from D. Soman, "The Mental Accounting of Sunk Time Costs: Why Time Is Not Like Money," *Journal of Behavioral Decision Making* 14, no. 3 (2001): 169–185.

58. H. Collins and A. V. Whillans, "Accounting for Time," hbr.org, January 30, 2019, https://hbr.org/2019/01/accounting-for-time.

59. S. Moore and J. P. Shepherd, "The Cost of Fear: Shadow Pricing the Intangible Costs of Crime," *Applied Economics* 38, no. 3 (2006): 293–300; N. Powdthavee, "Putting a Price Tag on Friends, Relatives, and Neighbours: Using Surveys of Life Satisfaction to Value Social Relationships," *Journal of Socio-Economics* 37, no. 4 (2008): 1459–1480; and N. Powdthavee and B. Van Den Berg, "Putting Different Price Tags on the Same Health Condition: Re-Evaluating the Well-Being Valuation Approach," *Journal of Health Economics* 30, no. 5 (2011): 1032–1043.

60. I am basing the income increase of happiness on my prior research showing that earning $10,000 more in household income was linked to a happiness boost of about 0.5 points on a 10-point happiness scale. I observed this income increase in a nationally representative sample of employed Americans living in the United States (*N*=1265). I also based my data on showing that people's happiness changes by about 0.5 points on a happiness scale from an experiment showing the direct happiness increase from buying time. Both studies are reported in A. V. Whillans, E. W. Dunn, P. Smeets, R. Bekkers, and M. I. Norton, "Buying Time Promotes Happiness," *Proceedings of the National Academy of Sciences* 114, no. 32 (2017): 8523–8527, study 9.

61. I chose to make the annual income in these examples $50,000 because this amount is slightly less than the median annual household income in the United States, according to the US Census Bureau, and it is a round number. The US Census Bureau reported that the median household income was $61,372 in 2018; https://www.census .gov/library/stories/2018/09/highest-median-household-income-on-record.html.

62. L. Giurge and A. V. Whillans, "Beyond Material Poverty: Why Time Poverty Matters for Individuals, Organisations, and Nations" (working paper, Harvard Business School, no. 20-051, 2020).

63. Study 4 of Whillans et al., "Valuing Time over Money Is Associated with Greater Happiness."

64. I. Dar-Nimrod, C. D. Rawn, D. R. Lehman, and B. Schwartz, "The Maximization Paradox: The Costs of Seeking Alternatives," *Personality and Individual Differences* 46, no. 5-6 (2009): 631–635.

65. Underlying data available upon request.

66. Whillans, "Time for Happiness: Why the Pursuit of Money Isn't Bringing You Joy—And What Will."

67. Nine out of ten consumers seek bargains when online shopping, a task that takes about thirty-two minutes: H. Leggatt, "Survey Reveals How Long Shoppers Spend Comparing Prices Online," *BizReport*, November 3, 2014, http://www.bizreport.com/2014/11 /survey-reveals-how-long-shoppers-spend-comparing-prices-online.html.

68. Collins and Whillans, "Accounting for Time."

69. N. Powdthavee, "Putting a Price Tag on Friends, Relatives, and Neighbours: Using Surveys of Life Satisfaction to Value Social Relationships," *Journal of Socio-Economics* 37, no. 4 (2008): 1459–1480.

## Chapter 3

1. A. Whillans, "Exchanging Cents for Seconds: The Happiness Benefits of Choosing Time over Money" (doctoral dissertation, University of British Columbia, 2017).

2. E. W. Dunn, A. V. Whillans, M. I. Norton, and L. B. Aknin, "Prosocial Spending and Buying Time: Money As a Tool for Increasing Well-Being," *Advances in Experimental Social Psychology* 61 (2020): 67–126.

3. S. E. Lea and P. Webley, "Money As Tool, Money As Drug: The Biological Psychology of a Strong Incentive," *Behavioral and Brain Sciences* 29, no. 2 (2006): 161–209.

4. K. D. Vohs, "Money Priming Can Change People's Thoughts, Feelings, Motivations, and Behaviors: An Update on 10 Years of Experiments," *Journal of Experimental Psychology: General* 144, no. 4 (2015): e86.

5. R. D. Horan, E. Bulte, and J. F. Shogren, "How Trade Saved Humanity from Biological Exclusion: An Economic Theory of Neanderthal Extinction," *Journal of Economic Behavior and Organization* 58, no. 1 (2005): 1–29.

6. Lea and Webley, "Money As Tool, Money As Drug: The Biological Psychology of a Strong Incentive."

7. In 2016, the Indian government removed 500- and 1,000-rupee bank notes. This decision was designed to reduce corruption. India is a cash economy, and at the time of the change, a large percentage of transactions were in notes of 500 rupees or more; thus, somewhat understandably, citizens were upset about the restriction of their use of these bills. "India Scraps 500 and 1,000 Rupee Bank Notes Overnight," BBC, November 9, 2016, https://www.bbc.com/news/business-37906742.

8. Y. Zhou, Y. Wang, L. L. Rao, L. Q. Yang, and S. Li, "Money Talks: Neural Substrate of Modulation of Fairness by Monetary Incentives," *Frontiers in Behavioral Neuroscience* 8 (2014): 150; C. C. Wu, Y. F. Liu, Y. J. Chen, and C. J. Wang, "Consumer Responses to Price Discrimination: Discriminating Bases, Inequality Status, and Information Disclosure Timing Influences," *Journal of Business Research* 65, no. 1 (2012): 106–116; and T. Kim, T. Zhang, and M. I. Norton, "Pettiness in Social Exchange," *Journal of Experimental Psychology: General* 148, no. 2 (2019): 361.

9. A. Gasiorowska, L. N. Chaplin, T. Zaleskiewicz, S. Wygrab, and K. D. Vohs, "Money Cues Increase Agency and Decrease Prosociality Among Children: Early Signs of Market-Mode Behaviors," *Psychological Science* 27, no. 3 (2016): 331–344. There is evidence that some of these experiments do not replicate, suggesting that there are factors that predict whether and when reminders of money shape our willingness to work versus help others. See E. M. Caruso, O. Shapira, and J. F. Landy, "Show Me the Money: A Systematic Exploration of Manipulations, Moderators, and Mechanisms of Priming Effects," *Psychological Science* 28, no. 8 (2017): 1148–1159.

10. H. E. Hershfield, C. Mogilner, and U. Barnea, "People Who Choose Time over Money Are Happier," *Social Psychological and Personality Science* 7, no. 7 (2016): 697–706.

11. T. Kasser, "Materialistic Values and Goals," *Annual Review of Psychology* 67 (2016): 489–514.

12. P. M. Gollwitzer, "Implementation Intentions: Strong Effects of Simple Plans," *American Psychologist* 54, no. 7 (1999): 493.

13. K. L. Milkman, J. Beshears, J. J. Choi, D. Laibson, and B. C. Madrian, "Using Implementation Intentions Prompts to Enhance Influenza Vaccination Rates," *Proceedings of the National Academy of Sciences* 108, no. 26 (2011): 10415–10420; K. L. Milkman, J. Beshears, J. J. Choi, D. Laibson, and B. C. Madrian, "Planning Prompts As a Means of Increasing Preventive Screening Rates," *Preventive Medicine* 56, no. 1 (2013): 92–93; D. W. Nickerson and T. Rogers, "Do You Have a Voting Plan? Implementation Intentions, Voter Turnout, and Organic Plan Making," *Psychological Science* 21, no. 2 (2010): 194–199; T. Rogers, K. L. Milkman, L. John, and M. I. Norton, "Making the Best-Laid Plans Better: How Plan Making Increases Follow-Through," *Behavioral Science and Policy* (2013); and T. Rogers, K. L. Milkman, L. K. John, and M. I. Norton, "Beyond Good Intentions: Prompting People to Make Plans Improves Follow-Through on Important Tasks," *Behavioral Science and Policy* 1, no. 2 (2015): 33–41.

14. K. E. Lee, K. J. Williams, L. D. Sargent, N. S. Williams, and K. A. Johnson, "40-Second Green Roof Views Sustain Attention: The Role of Micro-Breaks in Attention Restoration," *Journal of Environmental Psychology* 42 (2015): 182–189; and K. A. MacLean, E. Ferrer, S. R. Aichele, D. A. Bridwell, A. P. Zanesco, T. L. Jacobs, B. G.

King, et al., "Intensive Meditation Training Improves Perceptual Discrimination and Sustained Attention," *Psychological Science* 21, no. 6 (2010): 829–839.

15. N. Fitz, K. Kushlev, R. Jagannathan, T. Lewis, D. Paliwal, and D. Ariely, "Batching Smartphone Notifications Can Improve Well-Being," *Computers in Human Behavior* 101 (2019): 84–94.

16. A. V. Whillans and F. S. Chen, "Facebook Undermines the Social Belonging of First Year Students," *Personality and Individual Differences* 133 (2018): 13–16; and K. Burnell, M. J. George, J. W. Vollet, S. E. Ehrenreich, and M. K. Underwood, "Passive Social Networking Site Use and Well-Being: The Mediating Roles of Social Comparison and the Fear of Missing Out," *Cyberpsychology: Journal of Psychosocial Research on Cyberspace* 13, no. 3 (2019).

17. S. M. Schueller, "Personality Fit and Positive Interventions: Extraverted and Introverted Individuals Benefit from Different Happiness Increasing Strategies," *Psychology* 3, no. 12 (2012): 1166.

18. G. Tonietto and S. A. Malkoc, "The Calendar Mindset: Scheduling Takes the Fun Out and Puts the Work In," *Journal of Marketing Research* 53, no. 6 (2016): 922–936.

19. G. N. Tonietto, S. A. Malkoc, and S. M. Nowlis, "When an Hour Feels Shorter: Future Boundary Tasks Alter Consumption by Contracting Time," *Journal of Consumer Research* 45, no. 5 (2019): 1085–1102.

20. Ibid.

21. G. M. Sandstrom and E. W. Dunn, "Is Efficiency Overrated? Minimal Social Interactions Lead to Belonging and Positive Affect," *Social Psychological and Personality Science* 54, no. 4 (2014): 437–442.

22. M. S. Granovetter, "The Strength of Weak Ties," in *Social Networks*, ed. S. Leinhart (New York: Academic Press, 1977), 347–367; and M. Granovetter, "The Strength of Weak Ties: A Network Theory Revisited," *Sociological Theory* 1 (1983): 201–233.

23. A. L. Sellier and T. Avnet, "So, What If the Clock Strikes? Scheduling Style, Control, and Well-Being," *Journal of Personality and Social Psychology* 107, no. 5 (2014): 791.

24. T. Avnet and A. L. Sellier, "Clock Time vs. Event Time: Temporal Culture or Self-Regulation?" *Journal of Experimental Social Psychology* 47, no. 3 (2011): 665–667.

25. For a review, see A. L. Sellier and T. Avnet, "Scheduling Styles," *Current Opinion in Psychology* 26 (2019): 76–79.

26. T. Rogers and K. L. Milkman, "Reminders Through Association," *Psychological Science* 27, no. 7 (2016): 973–986.

27. C. Blank, L. M. Giurge, L. Newman, and A. Whillans, "Getting Your Team to Do More Than Meet Deadlines," hbr.org, November 15, 2019, https://hbr.org/2019/11/getting-your-team-to-do-more-than-meet-deadlines.

28. A. Thibault Landry and A. Whillans, "The Power of Workplace Rewards: Using Self-Determination Theory to Understand Why Reward Satisfaction Matters for Workers Around the World," *Compensation and Benefits Review* 50, no. 3 (2018): 123–148.

29. M. Kosfeld and S. Neckermann, "Getting More Work for Nothing? Symbolic Awards and Worker Performance," *American Economic Journal: Microeconomics* 3, no. 3 (2011): 86–99.

30. L. Shen, A. Fishbach, and C. K. Hsee, "The Motivating-Uncertainty Effect: Uncertainty Increases Resource Investment in the Process of Reward Pursuit," *Journal of Consumer Research* 41, no. 5 (2014): 1301–1315.

31. G. Grolleau, M. G. Kocher, and A. Sutan, "Cheating and Loss Aversion: Do People Cheat More to Avoid a Loss?" *Management Science* 62, no. 12 (2016): 3428–3438.

32. L. Pierce, A. Rees-Jones, and C. Blank, "The Negative Consequences of Loss-Framed Performance Incentives" (working paper, National Bureau of Economic Research, no. 26619, 2020).

33. For a summary of the latest technology applications that are helping people take back their time, see an article I wrote on the topic: "Our Smartphone Addiction Is Killing

Us: Can Apps That Limit Screen Time Offer a Lifeline?" *Conversation*, April 30, 2019, https://theconversation.com/our-smartphone-addiction-is-killing-us-can-apps-that-limit -screen-time-offer-a-lifeline-116220.

34. M. Zhu, Y. Yang, and C. K. Hsee, "The Mere Urgency Effect," *Journal of Consumer Research* 45, no. 3 (2018): 673–690.

35. C. Blank, L. M. Giurge, L. Newman, and A. Whillans, "Getting Your Team to Do More Than Meet Deadlines," hbr.org, November 15, 2019, https://hbr.org/2019/11 /getting-your-team-to-do-more-than-meet-deadlines.

36. S. E. DeVoe and J. House, "Time, Money, and Happiness: How Does Putting a Price on Time Affect Our Ability to Smell the Roses?" *Journal of Experimental Social Psychology* 48, no. 2 (2012): 466–474; J. House, S. E. DeVoe, and C. B. Zhong, "Too Impatient to Smell the Roses: Exposure to Fast Food Impedes Happiness," *Social Psychological and Personality Science* 5, no. 5 (2014): 534–541. There is some debate about the replicability of these findings. This study failed to show that putting a financial value on time undermines leisure enjoyment: S. Connors, M. Khamitov, S. Moroz, L. Campbell, and C. Henderson, "Time, Money, and Happiness: Does Putting a Price on Time Affect Our Ability to Smell the Roses?" *Journal of Experimental Social Psychology* 67 (2016): 60–64. However, studying time–money trade-offs among online workers who are willing to give away leisure for very small amounts of money might not be ideal. See S. E. DeVoe and J. House, "Replications with MTurkers Who Are Naïve Versus Experienced with Academic Studies: A Comment on Connors, Khamitov, Moroz, Campbell, and Henderson (2015)," *Journal of Experimental Social Psychology* 100, no. 67 (2016): 65–67. For a recent review of the current state of the literature, see S. E. DeVoe, "The Psychological Consequence of Thinking About Time in Terms of Money," *Current Opinion in Psychology* 26 (2019): 103–105.

37. J. Etkin, "The Hidden Cost of Personal Quantification," *Journal of Consumer Research* 42, no. 6 (2016): 967–984.

38. L. E. Aknin, E. W. Dunn, and M. I. Norton, "Happiness Runs in a Circular Motion: Evidence for a Positive Feedback Loop Between Prosocial Spending and Happiness," *Journal of Happiness Studies* 13, no. 2 (2012): 347–355. M. A. Cohn and B. L. Fredrickson, "In Search of Durable Positive Psychology Interventions: Predictors and Consequences of Long-Term Positive Behavior Change," *Journal of Positive Psychology* 5, no. 5 (2010): 355–366. B. L. Fredrickson, "The Broaden-and-Build Theory of Positive Emotions," *Philosophical Transactions of the Royal Society of London, Series B: Biological Sciences* 359, no. 1449 (2004): 1367–1377.

39. G. Loewenstein, "Hot-Cold Empathy Gaps and Medical Decision Making," *Health Psychology* 24, no. 4S (2005): S49. G. Loewenstein, "Emotions in Economic Theory and Economic Behavior," *American Economic Review* 90, no. 2 (2000): 426–432; and G. Loewenstein and D. Schkade, "Wouldn't It Be Nice? Predicting Future Feelings," *Well-Being: The Foundations of Hedonic Psychology* (1999): 85–105.

40. S. M. McCrea, "Self-Handicapping, Excuse Making, and Counterfactual Thinking: Consequences for Self-Esteem and Future Motivation," *Journal of Personality and Social Psychology* 95, no. 2 (2008): 274.

41. P. A. Siegel, J. Scillitoe, and R. Parks-Yancy, "Reducing the Tendency to Self-Handicap: The Effect of Self-Affirmation," *Journal of Experimental Social Psychology* 41, no. 6 (2005): 589–597.

## Chapter 4

1. A. Whillans, L. Macchia, and E. Dunn, "Valuing Time over Money Predicts Happiness after a Major Life Transition: A Preregistered Longitudinal Study of Graduating Students," *Science Advances* 5, no. 9 (2019): eaax2615.

2. K. Woolley and A. Fishbach, "The Experience Matters More Than You Think: People Value Intrinsic Incentives More Inside Than Outside an Activity," *Journal of Personality and Social Psychology* 109, no. 6 (2015): 968.

3. Whillans et al., "Valuing Time over Money Predicts Happiness after a Major Life Transition: A Preregistered Longitudinal Study of Graduating Students."

4. Woolley and Fishbach, "The Experience Matters More Than You Think: People Value Intrinsic Incentives More Inside Than Outside an Activity"; and A. A. Scholer, D. B. Miele, K. Murayama, and K. Fujita, "New Directions in Self-Regulation: The Role of Metamotivational Beliefs," *Current Directions in Psychological Science* 27, no. 6 (2018): 437–442.

5. A. V. Whillans, R. Dwyer, J. Yoon, and A. Schweyer, "From Dollars to Sense: Placing a Monetary Value on Non-Cash Compensation Encourages Employees to Value Time over Money" (working paper, Harvard Business School, no. 18-059, 2019).

6. Whillans, Dwyer, Yoon, and Schweyer, "From Dollars to Sense."

7. Americans spend twenty-six minutes commuting each way to work. C. Ingraham, "The Astonishing Human Potential Wasted on Commutes," *Washington Post*, February 25, 2016, https://www.washingtonpost.com/news/wonk/wp/2016/02/25/how-much-of-your-life -youre-wasting-on-your-commute/.

8. The participant who is quoted was interviewed for a research project conducted by Thrive Global. The full interview is available at The Money Mix, "Is Your Commute Making You Miserable?" *Thrive Global*, July 16, 2019, https://thriveglobal.com/stories/is -your-commute-making-you-miserable/.

9. Researchers often define commutes as a place for role transition, because they are the space between home and work life. See J. Jachimowicz, J. Lee, B. R. Staats, J. Menges, and F. Gino, "Between Home and Work: Commuting as an Opportunity for Role Transitions" (working paper, Harvard Business School NOM Unit, no. 16-077, 2019).

10. L. Karsten, "Housing As a Way of Life: Towards an Understanding of Middle-Class Families' Preference for an Urban Residential Location," *Housing Studies* 22, no. 1 (2007) 83–98; and M. Van der Klis and L. Karsten, "The Commuter Family As a Geographical Adaptive Strategy for the Work–Family Balance," *Community, Work and Family* 12, no. 3 (2009): 339–354.

11. H. Jarvis, "Moving to London Time: Household Co-Ordination and the Infrastructure of Everyday Life," *Time and Society* 14, no. 1 (2005): 133–154.

12. T. Schwanen and T. De Jong, "Exploring the Juggling of Responsibilities with Space-Time Accessibility Analysis," *Urban Geography* 29, no. 6 (2008): 556–580.

13. T. Schwanen, "Managing Uncertain Arrival Times Through Socio-Material Associations," *Environment and Planning B: Planning and Design* 35, no. 6 (2008): 997–1011, https://www.vtpi.org/ihasc.pdf.

14. J. Etkin and C. Mogilner, "Does Variety Among Activities Increase Happiness?" *Journal of Consumer Research* 43, no. 2 (2016): 210–229; and K. M. Sheldon, J. Boehm, and S. Lyubomirsky, "Variety Is the Spice of Happiness: The Hedonic Adaptation Prevention Model," in *Oxford Handbook of Happiness*, ed. I. Boniwell, S. A. David, and A. C. Ayers (Oxford: Oxford University Press, 2013), 901–914.

15. L. J. Levine and M. A. Safer, "Sources of Bias in Memory for Emotions," *Current Directions in Psychological Science* 11, no. 5 (2002): 169–173; and T. D. Wilson and D. T. Gilbert, "Affective Forecasting," *Advances in Experimental Social Psychology* 35, no. 35 (2003): 345–411.

16. K. Kushlev, S. J. Heintzelman, S. Oishi, and E. Diener, "The Declining Marginal Utility of Social Time for Subjective Well-Being," *Journal of Research in Personality* 74 (2018): 124–140.

17. Kushlev, Heintzelman, Oishi, and Diener, "The Declining Marginal Utility of Social Time for Subjective Well-Being."

18. A. M. Grant and B. Schwartz, "Too Much of a Good Thing: The Challenge and Opportunity of the Inverted U," *Perspectives on Psychological Science* 6, no. 1 (2011): 61–76.

19. R. Wiseman, *The Luck Factor* (New York: Random House, 2004).

20. R. Wiseman and C. Watt, "Measuring Superstitious Belief: Why Lucky Charms Matter," *Personality and Individual Differences* 37 (2004): 1533–1541.

21. Improvisation is being taught at top business schools in the United States, because it encourages people to be open to new ideas. For a course description, see Stanford Graduate School of Business, "Humor: Serious Business," nd, https://humor-seriousbusiness.stanford.edu/.

22. M. Akinola, A. E. Martin, and K. W. Phillips, "To Delegate or Not to Delegate: Gender Differences in Affective Associations and Behavioral Responses to Delegation," *Academy of Management Journal* 61, no. 4 (2018): 1467–1491; and L. Anik and M. I. Norton, "Matchmaking Promotes Happiness," *Social Psychological and Personality Science* 5, no. 6 (2014): 644–652.

23. E. W. Dunn, L. B. Aknin, and M. I. Norton, "Prosocial Spending and Happiness: Using Money to Benefit Others Pays Off," *Current Directions in Psychological Science* 23, no. 1 (2014): 41–47; and L. B. Aknin, A. V. Whillans, M. I. Norton, and E. W. Dunn, "Happiness and Prosocial Behavior: An Evaluation of the Evidence," *World Happiness Report* (2019).

24. G. Donnelly, A. V. Whillans, A. Wilson, and M. I. Norton, "Communicating Resource Scarcity" (working paper, Harvard Business School, no. 19-066, 2019).

25. J. Yoon, G. Donnelly, and A. V. Whillans, "It Doesn't Hurt to Ask (For More Time): Employees Often Overestimate the Interpersonal Costs of Extension Requests" (working paper, Harvard Business School, no. 19-064, 2019).

26. C. Fritz and S. Sonnentag, "Recovery, Well-Being, and Performance-Related Outcomes: The Role of Workload and Vacation Experiences," *Journal of Applied Psychology* 91, no. 4 (2006): 936.

27. S. Sonnentag, "Burnout Research: Adding an Off-Work and Day-Level Perspective," *Work and Stress* 19, no. 3, 2 (2005): 271–275; C. Fritz, S. Sonnentag, P. E. Spector, and J. A. McInroe, "The Weekend Matters: Relationships Between Stress Recovery and Affective Experiences," *Journal of Organizational Behavior* 31, no. 8 (2010): 1137–1162; and C. S. Dewa, D. Loong, S. Bonato, N. X. Thanh, and P. Jacobs, "How Does Burnout Affect Physician Productivity? A Systematic Literature Review," *BMC Health Services Research* 14, no. 1 (2014): 325.

28. For a review of the literature showing that employees should ask for more money and ways to go about it, see D. M. Kolb and J. L. Porter, *Negotiating at Work: Turn Small Wins into Big Gains* (New York: John Wiley & Sons, 2015); and D. Malhotra, "15 Rules for Negotiating a Job Offer," *Harvard Business Review*, April 2014.

29. M. T. Jensen, "Exploring Business Travel with Work–Family Conflict and the Emotional Exhaustion Component of Burnout As Outcome Variables: The Job Demands–Resources Perspective," *European Journal of Work and Organizational Psychology* 23, no. 4 (2014): 497–510.

30. M. Westman and D. Etzion, "The Impact of Short Overseas Business Trips on Job Stress and Burnout," *Applied Psychology* 51, no. 4 (2002): 582–592.

31. A. V. Whillans, A. C. Weidman, and E. W. Dunn, "Valuing Time over Money Is Associated with Greater Happiness," *Social Psychological and Personality Science* 7, no. 3 (2016): 213–222.

32. M. Wittmann and S. Lehnhoff, "Age Effects in Perception of Time," *Psychological Reports* 97, no. 3 (2005): 921–935.

33. M. Wittmann and M. P. Paulus, "Temporal Horizons in Decision Making," *Journal of Neuroscience, Psychology, and Economics* 2, no. 1 (2009): 1; and S. M. Janssen, M. Naka, and W. J. Friedman, "Why Does Life Appear to Speed Up As People Get Older?" *Time and Society* 22, no. 2 (2013): 274–290.

## Chapter 5

1. L. Giurge and A. V. Whillans, "Beyond Material Poverty: Why Time Poverty Matters for Individuals, Organisations, and Nations" (working paper, Harvard Business School, no. 20-051, 2020).

2. The best estimates of how much time paperwork burdens waste for US workers comes in at nearly $10 billion per year. C. R. Sunstein, "Sludge and Ordeals," *Duke Law Journal* 68 (2019): 1843.

3. The US Office of Information and Regulatory Affairs (OIRA)—the agency that oversees the implementation of government regulations—estimated that the paperwork burdens had grown to nearly 12 billion hours: https://www.reginfo.gov/public/do/PRAReport?operation=11.

4. A. Finkelstein and M. J. Notowidigdo, "Take-Up and Targeting: Experimental Evidence from SNAP," *Quarterly Journal of Economics* 134, no. 3 (2019): 1505–1556.

5. V. Alatas, R. Purnamasari, M. Wai-Poi, A. Banerjee, B. A. Olken, and R. Hanna, "Self-Targeting: Evidence from a Field Experiment in Indonesia," *Journal of Political Economy* 124, no. 2 (2016): 371–427.

6. A. Brodsky and T. M. Amabile, "The Downside of Downtime: The Prevalence and Work Pacing Consequences of Idle Time at Work," *Journal of Applied Psychology* 103, no. 5 (2018): 496.

7. D. U. Himmelstein et al., "A Comparison of Hospital Administrative Costs in Eight Nations: US Costs Exceed All Others by Far," *Health Affairs* 33, no. 9 (2014): 1586–1594.

8. Executives and business professionals spend an average of twenty-three hours a week (trapped) in meetings—up from ten hours a week in the 1960s. See S. G. Rogelberg, C. Scott, and J. Kello, "The Science and Fiction of Meetings," *MIT Sloan Management Review* 48, no. 2 (2007): 18–21; and S. G. Rogelberg, L. R. Shanock, and C. W. Scott, "Wasted Time and Money in Meetings: Increasing Return on Investment," *Small Group Research* 43, no. 2 (2012): 236–245.

9. M. E. Porter and N. Nohria, "How CEOs Manage Time," *Harvard Business Review*, July–August 2018.

10. J. Yoon, A. V. Whillans, and E. O'Brien, "Superordinate Framing Increases Task Motivation" (working paper, Harvard Business School, 2019), study 1.

11. J. Pfeffer and D. R. Carney, "The Economic Evaluation of Time Can Cause Stress," *Academy of Management Discoveries* 4, no. 1 (2018): 74–93.

12. J. Hur, A. Lee-Yoon, and A. V. Whillans, "Who Is More Useful? The Impact of Performance Incentives on Work and Personal Relationships" (working paper, Harvard Business School, 2018).

13. J. Pfeffer and S. E. DeVoe, "The Economic Evaluation of Time: Organizational Causes and Individual Consequences," *Research in Organizational Behavior* 32 (2012): 47–62.

14. For reviews, see S. E. DeVoe, "The Psychological Consequence of Thinking About Time in Terms of Money," *Current Opinion in Psychology* 26 (2019): 103–105; A. Li, K. Rong, J. Gao, F. Tan, and Y. Peng, "'Putting a Price on Time': Conception, Consequences and Its Psychological Mechanism," *Advances in Psychological Science* 23, no. 10 (2015): 1679–1687; and A. Lee-Yoon and A. V. Whillans, "Making Seconds Count: When Valuing Time Promotes Subjective Well-Being," *Current Opinion in Psychology* 26 (2019): 54–57.

15. About one in four employees in the United States receives no paid vacation. The United States is the only country in which the government doesn't guarantee that its workers receive paid vacation time. This is according to research conducted by the Center for Economic and Policy Research. The full report is available at http://cepr.net/documents/publications/nvn-summary.pdf.

16. C. Fritz and S. Sonnentag, "Recovery, Well-Being, and Performance-Related Outcomes: The Role of Workload and Vacation Experiences," *Journal of Applied Psychology* 91, no. 4 (2006): 936; and J. de Bloom, S. Ritter, J. Kühnel, J. Reinders, and S. Geurts, "Vacation from Work: A 'Ticket to Creativity'?: The Effects of Recreational Travel on Cognitive Flexibility and Originality," *Tourism Management* 44 (2014): 164–171.

17. C. West, C. Mogilner, and S. E. DeVoe, "Taking Vacation Increases Meaning at Work," proceedings of ACR 2017, *Advances in Consumer Research* 45 (2017): 63–67.

18. J. De Bloom, M. Kompier, S. Geurts, C. de Weerth, T. Taris, and S. Sonnentag, "Do We Recover from Vacation? Meta-Analysis of Vacation Effects on Health and Well-Being," *Journal of Occupational Health* 51 (2008): 13–25.

19. J. Kühnel, S. Sonnentag, and M. Westman, "Does Work Engagement Increase after a Short Respite? The Role of Job Involvement As a Double-Edged Sword," *Journal of Occupational and Organizational Psychology* 82, no. 3 (2009): 575–594.

20. J. Kühnel and S. Sonnentag, "How Long Do You Benefit from Vacation? A Closer Look at the Fade-Out of Vacation Effects," *Journal of Organizational Behavior* 32, no. 1 (2011): 125–143; and J. De Bloom, S. A. Geurts, T. W. Taris, S. Sonnentag, C. de Weerth, and M. A. Kompier, "Effects of Vacation from Work on Health and Well-Being: Lots of Fun, Quickly Gone," *Work and Stress* 24, no. 2 (2010): 196–216.

21. J. McCarthy, "Taking Regular Vacations Can Help Boost Americans' Well-Being," Gallup, December 30, 2014, https://news.gallup.com/poll/180335/taking-regular -vacations-may-help-boost-americans.aspx.

22. S. Sonnentag, "The Recovery Paradox: Portraying the Complex Interplay Between Job Stressors, Lack of Recovery, and Poor Well-Being," *Research in Organizational Behavior* 38 (2018): 169–185.

23. H. Collins and A. V. Whillans, "Accounting for Time," hbr.org, January 30, 2019, https://hbr.org/2019/01/accounting-for-time.

24. Of those that were unused, 236 million vacation days were forfeited completely, resulting in an estimated $70 billion in lost benefits. See the following reports: U.S. Travel Association, "Paid Time Off Trends in the U.S.," nd, https://www.ustravel.org /sites/default/files/media_root/document/Paid%20Time%20Off%20Trends%20Fact%20 Sheet.pdf; and U.S. Travel Association, "More Time Off, Less Time Used," nd, https:// www.ustravel.org/sites/default/files/media_root/document/NPVD19_FactSheet.pdf.

25. The cost of all cars bought in the United States in 2019 is $462 billion, per a recent estimate by JD Power: "US Auto Sales Down in 2019 but Still Top 17 Million for Fifth Consecutive Year," CNBC, January 6, 2020, https://www.cnbc.com/2020/01/06/us -auto-sales-down-in-2019-but-still-top-17-million.html.

26. In one survey of more than 2,000 US adults who were in full-time jobs, 70 percent said that even when they took a vacation they didn't disconnect from work. See B. Heitmann, "Your Workplace Guide to Summer Vacation," blog post, July 11, 2018, https:// blog.linkedin.com/2018/july/11/your-workplace-guide-to-summer-vacation.

27. N. Pasricha and S. Nigam, "What One Company Learned from Forcing Employees to Use Their Vacation Time," hbr.org, August 11, 2017, https://hbr.org/2017/08/what -one-company-learned-from-forcing-employees-to-use-their-vacation-time.

28. D. Kim, "Does Paid Vacation Leave Protect Against Depression Among Working Americans? A National Longitudinal Fixed Effects Analysis," *Scandinavian Journal of Work, Environment and Health* 45, no. 1 (2018): 22–32.

29. A. V. Whillans, E. W. Dunn, and M. I. Norton, "Overcoming Barriers to Time-Saving: Reminders of Future Busyness Encourage Consumers to Buy Time," *Social Influence* 13, no. 2 (2018): 117–124.

30. M. Fassiotto, C. Simard, C. Sandborg, H. Valantine, and J. Raymond, "An Integrated Career Coaching and Time-Banking System Promoting Flexibility, Wellness, and Success: A Pilot Program at Stanford University School of Medicine," *Academic Medicine: Journal of the Association of American Medical Colleges* 93, no. 6 (2018): 881–887.

31. Physicians' quotations from H. MacCormick, "Stanford's 'Time Banking' Program Helps Emergency Room Physicians Avoid Burnout," *Scope*, August 21, 2015, https:// scopeblog.stanford.edu/2015/08/21/stanfords-time-banking-program-helps-emergency -room-physicians-avoid-burnout/; and B. Schulte, "Time in the Bank: A Stanford Plan to Save Doctors from Burnout," August 20, 2015, https://www.washingtonpost.com/news /inspired-life/wp/2015/08/20/the-innovative-stanford-program-thats-saving-emergency -room-doctors-from-burnout/.

32. A. V. Whillans, R. Dwyer, J. Yoon, and A. Schweyer, "From Dollars to Sense: Placing a Monetary Value on Non-Cash Compensation Encourages Employees to Value Time over Money" (working paper, Harvard Business School, no. 18-059, 2019).

33. F. Gino, C. A. Wilmuth, and A. W. Brooks, "Compared to Men, Women View Professional Advancement As Equally Attainable, but Less Desirable," *Proceedings of the National Academy of Sciences* 112, no. 40 (2015): 12354–12359.

34. J. Yoon, G. Donnelly, and A. V. Whillans, "It Doesn't Hurt to Ask (For More Time): Employees Often Overestimate the Interpersonal Costs of Extension Requests" (working paper, Harvard Business School, no. 19-064, 2019).

35. People who take all of their paid vacations are more likely to be promoted. See "Time Off and Vacation Usage," U.S. Travel Association, nd, https://www.ustravel.org /toolkit/time-and-vacation-usage. This research is summarized in S. Achor, "Are the People Who Take Vacations the Ones Who Get Promoted?" hbr.org, June 12, 2015, https://hbr.org/2015/06/are-the-people-who-take-vacations-the-ones-who-get-promoted.

36. P. Choudhury, C. Foroughi, and B. Larson, "Work-from-Anywhere: The Productivity Effects of Geographic Flexibility" (working paper, Harvard Business School, Technology and Operations Mgt. Unit, no. 19–054, 2019).

37. I. Hirway, *Mainstreaming Unpaid Work: Time-Use Data in Developing Policies* (Oxford: Oxford University Press, 2017).

38. For more detail on how US policies shape decisions about childcare and disproportionately burden women, see Brigid Schulte's research—for example, "New America Care Report Finds Child Care Doesn't Work for Anyone," blog post, January 23, 2017, http://www.brigidschulte.com/2017/new-america-care-report-finds-child-care-doesnt -work-for-anyone/.

39. Data on time spent on medical paperwork are summarized in M. Sanger-Katz, "Hate Paperwork? Medicaid Recipients Will Be Drowning in It," *New York Times*, January 18, 2018.

40. Sunstein, "Sludge and Ordeals."

41. A. V. Whillans and C. West, "Alleviating Time Poverty Among the Working Poor" (working paper, Harvard Business School, 2020), https://www.aeaweb.org/conference /2020/preliminary/paper/3rf3SEb2.

42. M. Gates, "Time Poverty: The Gender Gap No One's Talking About," video, February 22, 2016, https://www.youtube.com/watch?v=y7SLIYh3MGw.

43. R. A. Easterlin, "Does Economic Growth Improve the Human Lot? Some Empirical Evidence," in *Nations and Households in Economic Growth: Essays in Honour of Moses Abramovitz*, ed. P. A. David and M. W. Reder (New York: Academic Press, 1974); R. Costanza, M. Hart, J. Talberth, and S. Posner, "Beyond GDP: The Need for New Measures of Progress," *Pardee Papers*, no. 4 (2009); E. Diener, S. Oishi, and R. E. Lucas, "National Accounts of Subjective Well-Being," *American Psychologist* 70, no. 3 (2015): 234; and J. F. Helliwell, "Well-Being, Social Capital and Public Policy: What's New?" *Economic Journal* 116, no. 510 (2006): C34–C45.

44. L. Macchia and A. V. Whillans, "Leisure Beliefs and the Subjective Well-Being of Nations," *Journal of Positive Psychology* (2019), doi:/full/10.1080/17439760.2019.168941.

45. Macchia and Whillans, "Leisure Beliefs and the Subjective Well-Being of Nations."

46. S. Lee, W. J. Guo, A. Tsang, A. D. Mak, J. Wu, K. L. Ng, and K. Kwok, "Evidence for the 2008 Economic Crisis Exacerbating Depression in Hong Kong," *Journal of Affective Disorders* 126, no. 1-2 (2010): 125–133.

47. Macchia and Whillans, "Leisure Beliefs and the Subjective Well-Being of Nations."

48. Ibid.

49. L. Alderman, "In Sweden, Experiment Turns Shorter Workdays into Bigger Gains," *New York Times*, May 20, 2016.

50. See https://www.empowerbus.com/.

51. Research showing that Americans lost an average of 97 hours a year due to congestion—which cost them nearly $87 billion in 2018, or an average of $1,348 per driver—is attributable to a calculation from INRIX, a mobility analytics firm. It arrived at this number by analyzing 500 terabytes of data from 300 million sources that covered more than 5 million miles of road. The data underlying this report involves the congested or uncongested status of every segment of road for every minute of the day (that relies on INRIX-based traffic services). For more information, see "INRIX: Congestion Costs Each American 97 Hours, $1348 a Year," INRIX, press release, February 11, 2019, https://inrix.com/press-releases/scorecard-2018-us/.

52. A. Smith, "Shared, Collaborative and on Demand: The New Digital Economy," Pew Research Center, press release, March 19, 2016.

53. A. S. Kristal and A. V. Whillans, "What We Can Learn from Five Naturalistic Field Experiments That Failed to Shift Commuter Behaviour," *Nature Human Behaviour* 4 (2020): 169–176.

54. Quotations in K. Clayton, "Be an Elegant Simplifier," *Behavioral Scientist*, February 7, 2019, https://behavioralscientist.org/be-an-elegant-simplifier/.

55. A. H. Petersen, "How Millennials Became the Burnout Generation," *BuzzFeed News,* January 5, 2019, https://www.buzzfeednews.com/article/annehelenpetersen/mille nnials-burnout-generation-debt-work.

## Conclusion

1. Robert H. Frank, *Under the Influence: Putting Peer Pressure to Work* (Princeton, NJ: Princeton University Press, 2020).

# INDEX

# ACKNOWLEDGMENTS

When I started writing this book as a first-year faculty member, I had conducted a lot of research showing that focusing on time—as opposed to money—was a productive path to greater happiness, better relationships, and improved physical health. Despite uncovering these research findings, my personal life was in shambles. My relationship with my partner of ten years fell apart because I too often chose work over relationships. I struggled to put the insights from my studies into practice. I was tired of always joking to "do what I say, not what I do" when it came to time-use decisions. If, armed with data, I was having such a hard time "walking the talk," certainly other people were struggling to navigate time and career decisions too. This book is my attempt to help myself and others put some of the academic research into practice each day. And I couldn't have succeeded in completing this book or conducting the underlying research without an entire community of supporters.

It started—as all manuscripts do—with an understanding and talented editor who "got it." Scott Berinato was there for me from day one. After numerous editors had turned me away, Scott saw the potential for these ideas to change how people think about and spend their time. He patiently taught me how to write in English instead of academese and to be more personal than I thought possible. From the initial draft of the HBR article that eventually became this manuscript to the final copy of the completed draft, he cheered me on. Scott was truly the best book Sherpa a first-time author could ever have. I will be forever grateful for Scott's guidance and am excited to continue being #TimeSmart together.

A lot of the research underlying this book was conducted in collaboration with some of the best mentors, colleagues, and students. First I want to thank my graduate school adviser, Elizabeth Dunn. I learned so much from her that I use every single day—both about happiness research and about how to be a socially aware and engaged scholar. I couldn't have written this book without her many years of encouragement. Mike Norton has also been a constant supporter of my research and of this book, and for that I am incredibly grateful. My colleague Heather Devine has provided a consistent stream of inspiration—to stay true to my values and to keep trying to get up every day and do research that makes a difference.

I want to thank my vast network of collaborators, supporters, and students: Raju Agarwal, Lara Aknin, Max Bazerman, Rene Bekkers, Saika Belal, Charlotte Blank, Eugene Caruso, Bill Chen, Frances Chen, Hanne Collins, Sanford DeVoe, Grant Donnelly, Ryan Dwyer, Holly Dykstra, Abby Falik, Laura Giurge, Liz Goldenberg, Antonya Gonzalez, Carol Graham, Andy Hafenbrack, Julia Hur, Jon Jachimowicz, Leslie John, Alex Jordan, Felicia Joy, Eric Kim, Ariella Kristal, Kostadin Kushlev, Matthew Lee, Alice Lee-Yoon, Lucia Macchia, Michael McGarrah, Cassie Mogilner, Cynthia Montgomery, Laurel Newman, Ed O'Brien, Shibeal O'Flaherty, Andrew Oswald, Mark Ottoni-Wilhelm, Lora Park, Leslie Perlow, Jessica Pow, Nattavudh (Nick) Powdthavee, Jason Proulx, Jessica Roberts, Todd Rogers, Michael Sanders, Gillian Sandstrom, Laurie Santos, Allan Schweyer, Scott Seider, Joey Sherlock, Paul Smeets, Anaïs Thibault-Landry, Tyler VanderWeele, Kathleen Vohs, Deborah Ward, George Ward, Colin West, Ayse Yemisicigil, and Jaewon Yoon, to name a few. All of my colleagues have pushed this work in fascinating directions, and most of the research I discuss is a direct result of our collaborations and conversations. This book has also benefited from numerous conversations with scholars and practitioners in my department and at lab meetings, conferences, and seminars. The best part of my job is having impassioned conversations about ideas with smart people from diverse backgrounds and perspectives. For these conversations I am eternally grateful.

My research has been generously funded by numerous agencies, including Harvard Business School, Harvard University's Mind Brain Behavior Interfaculty Initiative, Harvard University's Pershing Square Fund for Research on the Foundations of Human Behavior, Harvard University's Burke Global Health Fellowship at the Harvard Global Health Institute, the John Templeton Foundation, the Lakshmi Mittal and Family South Asia Institute at Harvard University, the Social Sciences and Humanities Research Council of Canada, the UCLA Anderson School of Management, the IZA Institute for Labor Economics, and the London Business School. Without the support of these organizations my research and this book would not have been possible.

I would also like to thank my family: my mom, Lisa, my aunts and uncles, Peggy and Terry and Joan and Dean, and my cousins, Marc and Paul. In the face of a great deal of hardship, you have always managed to find time to laugh and be grateful. Special thanks to my dad, Brian. I always say that you are the true scientist because you approach life with an incredible sense of wonder. Your weekly phone calls about the latest interesting story from the internet or from one of my "academic magazines" remind me never to stop looking around and being amazed.

Last but not least, thanks to my partner, Umair. You have taught me what unconditional love and support looks like. From our Boston Public Library dates (where I thought you also had important work to do, but as it turns out, you were just coming with me to make sure I got my writing done) to cooking dinner when I was working under deadline to making sure I wasn't traveling too much, you always give me your unwavering support. You and Ollie (our kitty) make me feel grateful for every single moment of every day that we spend together. Now that we are a family, I can't imagine *not* living a time-focused life.

I wasn't supposed to be an academic, let alone an assistant professor at Harvard. I'm a first-generation college student. I dropped out of college the first time around and failed all my classes. Before I went to college (the second time), I had never met anyone who had graduated from university. The process of writing this book and pursuing a research career has taught me that you should never be afraid to aim high and go after your dreams. The worst that can happen is that you spend every moment in the pursuit of something you care deeply about, surrounded by people who care as much about these dreams as you do. I can't think of a better way to live out our limited lives: by spending each second in pursuit of something greater than ourselves. I hope this book serves as a reminder that how we spend our time is how we live our lives and that it helps us reconnect to our purpose and our why.

Now that I have written my first book, I'm looking forward to the next one. The future is increasingly uncertain, and time affluence could help us find solutions to many of the problems we face as a society, so long as we start taking time seriously.

# ABOUT THE AUTHOR

**Ashley Whillans** is an assistant professor at Harvard Business School, where she studies how people navigate trade-offs between time and money and how those decisions affect job satisfaction, happiness, and overall well-being. She has twice been named a Rising Star of Behavioral Science and has been published in numerous academic journals. Whillans is also passionate about science communication and public engagement with scientific research. She has been published by *Harvard Business Review*, the *New York Times*, the *Wall Street Journal*, and the *Washington Post*, and her work also has been featured in the *Atlantic*, the *Economist*, and on CNN and the BBC. Prior to HBS, she cofounded the Department of Behavioral Science in the Policy, Innovation, and Engagement Division of the British Columbia Public Service. She received a PhD in social psychology from the University of British Columbia.